**MY
FIRST 77
YEARS**

MY
FIRST 77
YEARS

By MONROE "MONK" PARKER

SWORD of the LORD
PUBLISHERS
P.O.BOX 1099, MURFREESBORO, TN 37133

PRINTED AND BOUND IN THE UNITED STATES OF AMERICA

Dedication

*This book is lovingly dedicated to the memory
of my parents, Weldon Jacob Parker and Lucy
E. Moseley Parker, whose prayers and godly
influence brought me to Christ and have
sustained me for seventy-seven years through
sunshine and shadows.*

Preface

I have been urged by many friends to write the story of my life. I have hesitated to do so.

I once read the life story of a street preacher by the name of Robert E. Lee Duckworth, Jr. He said that he started out from his home as a hobo riding on a freight train. The train stopped at Cottonwood, Mississippi, and he decided to go uptown and find out how far he had come from Columbus. When he started back to the train, he heard the "high-ball," the two little toots the whistle on the caboose gives when the train is pulling out of town; so Duckworth missed his train.

The Apostle Paul wrote, "Brethren, I count not myself to have apprehended: but this one thing I do, forgetting those things which are behind, and reaching forth unto those things which are before, I press toward the mark for the prize of the high calling of God in Christ Jesus" (Phil. 3:14, 15).

However, just as many of the experiences that Paul did recall and write about are a blessing to us, so it occurred to me that God's gracious dealings with me and His choice to use one so unworthy as I might be a blessing to many. It may encourage some young people to be resigned to the will of God and others to seek His will.

So with much prayer I set out to write my autobiography. I greatly appreciate the encouragement of many friends in this task. Especially I am grateful to Mrs. Jo Ann Huggins, my secretary who typed the original manuscript and retyped it after many alterations, additions, and insertions.

I am also grateful to Mrs. Ed (Guyla) Nelson for proofreading and helping me to reorganize it; for typing it into her computer to facilitate the typesetting.

Without confession to all of my sins, foibles, and failures, I have told as accurately as my fallible memory permitted as God has led me through sunshine and shadows.

John Monroe "Monk" Parker

Foreword

I have just read *Through Sunshine and Shadows* by Dr. Monroe Parker. I laughed—I cried—I praised the Lord—and I examined my own life.

Dr. Parker has been my hero since the first day I walked into the Preacher Boys' Class at Bob Jones College in January of 1946. He directed the class and challenged me to give my all to the ministry of the Word of God.

Every year Dr. Parker would spend some time just telling us "preacher boys" many of the experiences recorded in this autobiography. I am confident all of my classmates (and our class had 1100 preacher boys) would agree with me that the highlight of each year was the time we would have the privilege of hearing these thrilling stories.

My reading of the manuscript has been exciting, for I had the opportunity of reliving my days in class and the blessing of sitting under Monroe Parker's ministry.

In this book Dr. Parker has opened his heart to us. Now he is often referred to as the "Dean of Evangelists" in America. He is truly a great man who has been mightily and widely used of God. But here in this book we see those things that make a great man: trusting God to provide so that he can have a pair of shoes or two five-cent hamburgers; kneeling heartbroken by a dying wife following a tragic car accident; facing the trials and tests of each day with an unswerving faith that the Lord's will is best; rejecting the possibility of a pastorate with "an attractive salary and a lovely parsonage" to accept the challenge of a missionary spirit and go to Bevier, Kentucky, where all he had promised to him was a bed.

As a young man he was widely and mightily used of God—the Bevier-Cleaton, Kentucky, revival being a prime example. But he did not preach just in difficult fields like Bevier. As a young man he also had the privilege of speaking in the well-known and great churches of America such as Tremont Temple, Boston, and Moody Memorial Church, Chicago.

Now he is no longer a young man. But you can sense the vitality of a youthful mind at seventy-seven years of age. He is a man who has stood solidly for the Word of God, has preached with Holy Spirit power, and has maintained a non-compromising position when his peers were capitulating to the traps Satan was baiting.

In this autobiography you will see God's man remaining true and walking humbly whether he was a fervent, hard-hitting evangelist; a college administrator making the tough decisions daily while training thousands to go out in the harvest fields; a faithful pastor loving his people; or a missions director carrying the burden of unsaved billions on his heart and praying faithfully for every missionary associated with Baptist World Mission around the world. Here is the life story of a man, not just great in the eyes of those who have known his ministry but also in the eyes of the Lord of harvest.

I am sure you will thrill with me at the power of God to convert rebellious sinners. Today we all need to realize anew the revival power that is available to the church. I thank God that I have had the privilege of knowing Dr. Monroe Parker—and now that I have been able to relive with him a rich and full life dedicated to the Lord.

America's "Dean of Evangelists" has opened his heart to all of us. Thanks, Dr. Parker, for leaving us this legacy of blessing.

As you embark on this life journey with Monroe Parker, I am

sure you will feel the same pulse and heartbeat that challenged me as I read the manuscript. In this book we can realize that here is a man who has spoken unto us the Word of God, and we can confidently obey Hebrews 13:7—"...whose faith follow...."

Ed Nelson
Pastor, South Sheridan Baptist Church
Denver, Colorado

.

Table of Contents

CHAPTER I

Parker's Pedigree

W hen one tells the story of his life, he is supposed to begin with some statement of his pedigree. I will have to admit that I descended from Adam and Eve, who ate the forbidden fruit and brought us all into the vale of sin and woe and death. I therefore cannot claim that all of my forebears were altogether perfect, but I was blessed with a good family tree.

Paternal Pedigree

My paternal great, great grandfather, Uriah Parker, was a judge in Waycross, Georgia. He was a man of no mean reputation. His son, W. Jacob Parker, moved from Georgia to Alabama, where in 1843 he founded one of the first Baptist churches in that state, Shiloh Baptist Church in Choctaw County.

W. Jacob Parker had two sons, both of whom were Baptist preachers: my great uncle George and my grandfather, William Albert Parker.

A Preacher Family

Grandfather pastored several churches in Alabama and in 1903 organized the First Baptist Church of Thomasville. His wife, Sue Williamson, was from Lower Peachtree. To this couple were born eight sons and three daughters.

The daughters were Goodwin, who married a Baptist preacher,

Rev. George Mize; Emma, who married a Baptist preacher, Rev. George Cranford; and Eula, who was never married.

Gary

One of my father's brothers was Gary, who died as a little child. With the exception of my father, all of the other boys in his family were preachers. My father was not a preacher, but he was one of the best men I ever knew. He was a deacon.

Albert

Uncle Albert Parker pastored a number of churches in Alabama, including First Baptist Church, Collinsville, and First Baptist Church, Centre. He was also pastor in Mt. Enterprise, Texas, where he succeeded my grandfather, who died while pastor there in 1914.

William

Uncle William lived in Whistler, Alabama, where he did some preaching, although he worked in the railroad shop.

Jacob

My father was the third son and, like his grandfather, was named W. Jacob. He was not called W. Jacob II, however, because his first initial was for Weldon while his grandfather's was for William. My father was called W. J. and Jake.

Joseph

Uncle Joe pastored a number of churches in Texas and in Alabama. He was pastor in Vernon, Alabama, when God called him home.

Fox and John

Uncle L. L. Fox Parker and Uncle John M. Parker pastored churches in Texas. Both of them preached the Gospel for more than fifty years.

Douglas and Son

Uncle Douglas died while pastor of the Baptist church at Munson, Florida. His oldest son, Dr. Henry Allen Parker, has served as pastor of the Alapata Baptist Church, Miami; First Baptist Church, Dothan; First Baptist Church, Montgomery; and recently retired while pastor of First Baptist Church, Orlando.

Naturally, one with such an array of personalities on his paternal pedigree could write many volumes about them. Before turning to my maternal background, which is equally dramatic, I will mention that several of my cousins are in the ministry.

My Brother Jim

Preaching runs in the Parker blood. My brother, James W. Parker, a 1936 graduate of Bob Jones University and the first alumnus to receive the honorary degree Doctor of Divinity from that institution, pastored the First Baptist Church, Menlo, Georgia, 1937-39; Jackson Hill Baptist Church, Atlanta, 1940-43; First Baptist Church, Gonzales, Texas, 1943-50; Garden Oaks Baptist Church, Houston, 1950-65; and Bristol Street Baptist Church, Santa Ana, California, from 1965 until God called him home to Heaven May 22, 1976. God blessed him with an outstanding and fruitful ministry. Two of his three sons are preachers, and the other is in the ministry of music.

Maternal Pedigree

My maternal grandfather, Mr. Louis Lee Moseley, farmed two

sections of land near Thomasville, Alabama. He also owned and operated with his two eldest sons the largest grocery and meat market in the area. He was converted before his marriage and was a devout Christian and member of the First Baptist Church in Thomasville.

Although he was not a very large man, he was as strong as a mule and was a dynamic personality. When he became angry, as he often did, servants, members of his large family, and anyone else who happened to be around, stood at attention.

One funny incident which I remember vividly occurred at my grandfather's place. At eight o'clock each night in the winter, Grandpa would arise from his chair in front of a large, open fireplace and say, "Well, I will go and lie down a little while." He then went to his room and lay down and stayed eight hours. When the big grandfather clock in the hall struck four in the morning, he would get up and go out to milk several cows. One morning as he started out, his hat was not hanging in its usual place on the hall tree, but Aunt Jennie's hat was there. We were all awakened by my mother at dawn to look out the window and see Grandpa coming up the lane carrying two big pails of milk, wearing Aunt Jennie's large, purple hat with an ostrich plume on it.

Grandmother was a brilliant, consecrated Methodist. She was not a pietist but was devout. Her maiden name was Josephine Penelope Adams. She bore my grandfather fourteen children. They were as follows:

1. Jennie, who married Mr. Rufus Allen, Sheriff of Clark County, Alabama. Aunt Jennie lived to be over ninety years of age. Her last years were spent in Houston, Texas, where her four children lived. Her two sons, R. G. and Harry, were lawyers.

2. Fanny, who married Mr. Tom Kimbrough. They had three sons, Hubert Kimbrough of Mobile, an investment broker; the late Dr. Ralph Kimbrough, who practiced medicine in Birmingham over fifty years; and Earl, deceased.

3. Robert, who was in business with his father and later was in the shoe business in Decatur, Alabama.

My mother, back row center, with three of her sisters, two
of her sisters-in-law, and two of her brothers. (1952)

4. Cora, who married Mr. Charles Wilson of Ensley, co-owner of the Wilson-Clark Shoe Stores. Their children are Bell Cooper, wife of a Birmingham dentist; Lucille Blalock; and Dr. Charles Wilson, orthopedic surgeon, deceased. Lucille's son Harry is also an orthopedic surgeon, practicing in Birmingham.

5. Aunt Leona, who married Dr. Eugene Stutts, the dentist in Thomasville. They had three children; the first was Russell, who was an oral surgeon in Birmingham. He married Nellie Parker, sister of my second wife, whose maiden name was Parker. The second Stutts child was William, a lumberman in Thomasville; and the third was Mamie Jo, who married an attorney-at-law and is now a widow living in Highland, North Carolina.

6. William, who was in business for many years with his father and brother, Robert. Uncle Will was quite an entrepreneur. He was involved in many enterprises in Birmingham, where he resided for many years. Later he moved to Cordova, Alabama, where he had a store.

7. The seventh Moseley child was Lucy, my mother.

8. The eighth was Monroe, who died a few days before I was born. He was named for his maternal grandfather, Monroe Adams, and his name was passed on to me, along with the name of my uncle, John Parker. Although my name is John Monroe Parker, I have always been called by my middle name.

9. Coral, who married Mr. Micky Walker of Meridian, Mississippi. Mr. Walker passed away when Aunt Coral's two children were young. After the death of my Aunt Cora Wilson, Aunt Coral married Cora's widowed husband, Charles Wilson.

10. Frank, who was a pharmacist and automobile dealer in Panama City, Florida. When I was a teenage boy, Uncle Frank operated a drugstore in Thomasville.

11. Jessie, who married Mr. Pope of Grenada, Mississippi.

12. Leslie, who was a dentist, a long-time resident and mayor of Uniontown, Alabama.

13. Clayton, who died as a young man in his thirties.

14. Marcita, the youngest Moseley child, who married William

Dansby, attorney-at-law and banker, Butler, Alabama.

Many pages could be written about these interesting relatives and their numerous offsprings whom I have not mentioned for lack of space. So I will let my pedigree rest here except for occasional references to some of these relatives and many references to my parents.

My father, W. Jacob Parker, and my mother, Lucy E. Moseley, were married at Thomasville in 1905. On January 10, 1907, God blessed their union with the birth of my brother, Louis A., who was called Lew. My father worked in a clothing store in those days. Later he became marshal in Thomasville and owned and operated the Thomasville Hotel.

CHAPTER II

Birth and Childhood in Thomasville

My father built the house where I was born, and I was told that he rushed up the construction so that I could be born there early—June 23, 1909. We moved from that house when I was four years old, but I clearly remember many incidents that took place in and around my first home.

I Remember

I remember the excitement that prevailed when the two daughters of the Methodist minister, who lived across the street from us, took me to their home before I was two years old. They gave me a box of trinkets to play with but did not know that it contained some poison pills. The excitement took place when I swallowed one of those pills. I remember their rushing me home and the doctor's working frantically to save my life. This is my earliest recollection. I remember a man with a grind organ and a dancing bear appearing in front of our house for a performance.

I remember the Negro girl Carlene, who was called my "nurse." She baby-sat with me and looked after me until I was five years old. She used to take me down to the front steps of the Methodist church about two blocks away and visit with some of her friends who were also caring for little children whom they brought there.

Carlene was a faithful friend. After the death of my father in 1947, my mother moved back to Thomasville. There she and my

Monroe, age 1½, and Lew, age 4. (1911)

Monroe, age 4. "I had my picture took." (1913)

Aunt Coral, also widowed, rented and lived in the house where I was born. When Carlene would hear that I was coming to see Mother, she would ask Mother to let her come over and cook a meal for me. The last time I saw the dear old woman was the day of my mother's funeral. She came and asked what she could do to help. We mingled our tears, Lew and I hugged the old white-haired black woman, and I prayed with her. She is now in Heaven.

When I Was Four Years Old

When I was four years old, one day my mother said to me, "I want you to have your picture taken the next time you go to town."

Now for picture-taking, Mother always dressed us "fit to kill," as can be seen in the picture of my brother Lew and me when Lew was four and I was one and a half. The day after mother had said she wanted me to have my picture taken the next time I went to town, she sent me down to the market for a box of soda. I was in my play clothes and not dressed for picture-taking. But this was the next time I went to town. After so long a time that Mother was worried and started to go after me, I showed up and said, "Well, I had my picture took."

The result is seen in the picture in which I am standing in the same straw chair in Mr. Anderson's studio in which all of his subjects sat or stood.

One day when I was four years old, I followed some older boys into a watermelon patch that belonged to Mr. Hill, a roly-poly jolly man with a white mustache who reminded me of the fabled man of "The Night Before Christmas." Mr. Hill caught us and made us bring the melons we had plucked into his yard, where there was a long picnic table. He got a big butcher knife and cut the melons and let us eat them while he lectured to us on the sin of stealing.

From my earliest recollections, I was a God-conscious child. Another incident occurred when I was four which made an impression on my young mind. While running, I stepped on a broken bottle which cut straight across my left foot all the way to the bone.

Dr. John Kimbrough, our family doctor who delivered me when I was born, and got the poison out of me before I was two, and doctored me when I had diphtheria at the age of three, patched up my foot.

My mother took me with my sore left foot in a buggy out to my grandmother's to stay for a while. I was hopping around on my right foot near the barns and hopped on a nail which stuck deep into my foot. Hearing my loud screams, Grandmother came out with a washpan, a kettle of hot water, soap, a towel, a bottle of turpentine, some cotton, a big kitchen spoon, and some matches. This was standard first-aid equipment for her and also for my mother. After Grandmother washed and dried my foot, she dug a little hole in the ground with the spoon, saturated the cotton in turpentine, put it down in the hole, set it afire, and held my foot over it so that the smoke could go into the wound.

God Speaks to a Four-Year-Old Boy

Then Grandmother got me up on the high back porch, set me on a high stool, and gave me a ripe pear and a bunch of grapes. The tears were almost dry when suddenly a heavy iron bedstead, which had been leaning on the wall behind, fell over and struck the back of my head, knocked me off that stool, and scattered my fruit to the turkeys. I was angry with God, when out of the sky that had been clear a moment before, there came a clap of thunder loud enough to wake the dead. I looked up, and across the dark pavilion of a storm cloud, I saw a display of forked lightning such as I have seldom seen since. This was no mere coincidence; it was God speaking to a four-year-old boy. I knew I was a sinner. I did not get saved at that time; but I learned not to blame God, and I lay with my two injured feet and a knot on my head in reverential awe.

CHAPTER III

The Thomasville Hotel

My father had become the marshal in Thomasville and had purchased the Thomasville Hotel, a large frame mansion up the hill from the depot. We moved from the house my father built to a lovely house known as the annex to the hotel, large enough to accommodate us and occasional extra hotel guests. The depot was a social center in those days. Most of the able-bodied citizens of the town gathered at the depot four times a day when the passenger trains came in. This was not only to watch the trains come in and to see who would get off and who would be going out of town but also to enjoy a social time. This was especially true before the 6:00 P.M. train. For most of the ladies and girls, this was a dress-up occasion. They did not dress formally, but they wore fresh, pretty dresses. Some of the young men and boys spruced up a bit, too.

After the train pulled out, many people would follow the big carts of mail as they were pushed a block and a half to the post office. There the people would continue their visiting until the mail was "up"; that is, in the mail boxes.

Thomasville was a peaceful little town, but my father was marshal and had to put people in the calaboose. Sometimes he received threats of various kinds. When I was five years old, somebody carried out a threat and burned down our house, the annex. We then moved into the hotel.

CHAPTER IV

Boyhood in Texas

U pon the death of Grandfather Parker, who was pastor of the Baptist church in Mount Enterprise, Texas, we moved to Texas. We stayed with Grandmother Parker a few weeks until Uncle Albert was called to succeed his father as pastor in Mount Enterprise. Then we moved to Edgewood, Texas, where my father went into the haberdashery business.

In Edgewood I started to school in "Miss Lilly" Brannon's kindergarten. My first day in school was March 31, 1915, the day my brother Jimmy was born. When school was out at the end of May, I had learned to read. So when I went to grade school in September, I was placed in the second grade. If there is a deficiency in my education, it is because I never went to the first grade!

When I left home for the half-mile trek to kindergarten that first day, I started rolling a little wheel with a paddle. About halfway there I encountered a flock of guineas, creatures I had never seen before. They looked a little like chickens but made such a strange noise that I took out for home as fast as my little wheel would roll. My father had to leave my mother's bedside and take me past the guineas. After this I had no fear of those queer-looking fowls.

Often since those early years I have called upon my heavenly Father to go with me through some fearful experience, and His presence always dispels all fears. "Perfect love casteth out fear" (I John 4:16).

Once just before I was six years old, I was sent to the icehouse to get a nickel's worth of ice. On the way home I encountered Mr. Love West, a lawyer, who offered me a nickel to sit on the little block of ice until it melted. I took for granted that he would give me another nickel to replace the ice. I put the little block of ice down in the hot sand and sat on it. The ice began to melt. Since this was a cold business deal, I decided to ask Mr. West if he would pay for the ice. When he said he would not, I got up and took home what was left of the ice. My father spanked me, but I was too numb to feel it much. I learned from that experience to read the fine print of a contract, especially when dealing with a lawyer.

The Best Place to Rear Boys

Dad had an idea that a farm was the best place for boys to be reared. He bought a small farm a mile outside Edgewood, and we moved there in the summer of 1915. My brother Lew and I worked with the hired man, planted corn and potatoes, picked berries, chopped and picked cotton, and did other necessary jobs.

We also rode the horses and became full-fledged Texans. When I was six, I used to ride Old Ben, a large, gentle plow horse. I often rode him bareback and would occasionally fall off. He would follow me and stand by the side of a fence to let me climb up on the fence and get over on his bare back. I felt quite grown up at the age of six when I was allowed to ride alone to the grist mill with a sack of corn and bring back the cornmeal.

We had a creek on the farm where we used to swim in immodest fashion, shielded by a row of willow trees. We had a homemade boat that would sometimes stay afloat several minutes if we would bail fast enough. We fished in the creek and caught "crawdads" and a few perch and catfish.

December 18, 1916, a fourth son, Edwin, was born to my parents.

We Move to the Panhandle

My father's haberdashery business was very successful until practically all of the young men in town were called to arms in 1917, and Uncle Sam took over the job of furnishing their wardrobe. So Dad sold out, and we moved to Chillicothe in the lower Texas panhandle, where we lived until the fall of 1922. There my father managed the shoe department of a large dry goods store. He later became store manager.

These were difficult times for my family and for everyone else, for that matter. The first World War brought sorrow to the whole world. But it was a very patriotic time for America. We had wheatless days and meatless days and sugarless days. I did not mind the wheatless days as much as my parents because I was fond of pancakes made with cornmeal instead of flour. We always had a big garden and also raised a couple of hogs every year, as did nearly everyone else in little towns in the first part of this century. And we kept a cow which I used to lead to pasture every day.

I did not know that we were poor; but when I remember that I had a tumbleweed for a pet, I suppose we were. When I would fail to tie it up, I would have to chase it all over the school yard, which was across the street from our house. When the wind was just right, it would follow me for miles.

During World War I when so many men were "Over There," we boys "hired out" to pick cotton at $2.50 per hundred pounds. When I was nine years old, I made enough money to buy a bicycle. Then I could ride my own bike to Wanders Creek, and Lew did not have to "pump" me; that is, haul me on the rod of his bike.

In the panhandle the land is flat. You can ride for miles without the sight of a hill or a tree. In the springtime the wheat fields look like a great green gulf, and in the fall they look like a sea of gold. The summers are hot and dusty, and the heat waves shimmer above the fields like dancing film. Wheat shocking was done by hand when I was a lad, and we worked until we were almost "white eyed."

Except for a few little locust trees and some fruit trees and mesquite bushes, the only trees in the area lined the banks of Wanders Creek, which meandered about two miles west of town. Here we boys had a natural swimming place with a gypsum rock bottom deep enough to dive into from the trees. We spent many a happy day as young Tarzans swinging from tree to tree and into the creek below. And I might add, we sustained many a minor injury. An oak limb grew about twelve feet above the deepest part of the creek, and one was a coward if he did not dive from that limb at least two or three times during a swim. We used to take our .22 rifles out to the creek and hunt. The plains were inhabited with horned frogs, prairie dogs, jack rabbits, coyotes, badgers, hoot owls, and rattlesnakes; but along the creek were cottontails, squirrels, quail, ducks, and other game. We bagged squirrels and cottontail rabbits but never a jackrabbit.

"I Shot a Jackrabbit," Said I

One day when I had been out alone, I announced falsely at the supper table that I had shot a jackrabbit.

"What did you do with it?" asked the family in unison.

"Oh, I just left it out on the prairie," said I.

Jackrabbits are too tough to eat; so why should I have bothered to bring such a trophy home? Besides there were no taxidermists in my family!

"Just where on the prairie did you leave it?" asked my father, who suspected I was lying.

I said, "About a hundred yards from the Quanah highway and about fifty yards from Wanders Creek."

The next day was Sunday, and in the afternoon we went for a ride in our Ford sedan. There were no paved or even gravel roads near Chillicothe; and if we rode on a well-graded road, we had to go either toward Vernon or toward Quanah. My father chose Quanah; and when we were about fifty yards from Wanders Creek bridge, he stopped the car and said, "Mon, run out there and see if you can find that jackrabbit you killed yesterday."

I said, "The coyotes or the buzzards have probably eaten him, but I will go and see." I trotted about a hundred yards from the road, and there by a prickly pear cactus lay a dead jackrabbit. The devil or somebody certainly cooperated with a nine-year-old liar.

My folks seemed satisfied when they saw the carcass which I dragged back to the fence. Dad said, "Leave it there! We see it."

Several times afterward they told people that I killed a jackrabbit with a .22 rifle. This always embarrassed me, and I said as little about it as possible. The matter was dropped, and I thought forgot, until I became a preacher. Then one day my father said, "Mon, now that you are a preacher, you would not tell a lie, would you?"

I said, "It's not because I am a preacher but because I am a Christian I would not tell a lie."

Then he asked, "Did you kill that jackrabbit?"

I said, "I refuse to answer on the grounds that I lied." How true is the Bible verse, "Be sure your sin will find you out" (Num. 32:23)!

Happy Though Sad Times

The year 1918 was a happy though sad time for us. Happy because the great war ended with victory for the Allies. Sad because of sickness and death. I was stricken with paratyphoid in the early part of that year and spent six weeks in bed. Except for missing out on the fun others were having—like when a big snow came and all the neighborhood kids were making snowmen, and I was languishing in bed—the worst part of it was doing without food. My fever was very high, and the doctor said that I should have nothing to eat except mellins food, a malt mixture in water. I think if Mother had not gone out to take my brother James' picture in the snow, I would have starved to death. While she was out, I got out of bed and slipped into the kitchen where I found some baked sweet potatoes and some cold biscuits. I ate a yam and a biscuit and hurriedly took a yam and a biscuit to bed with me for later consumption. Afterwards, I made other raids on the kitchen "safe" (cabinet). I believe it was this nourishment that made me well. From the time I ate that first yam, I began to improve. Soon thereafter I was well.

The aforementioned bicycle, which I ordered and paid for with my cotton-picking money, came while I was in bed. This helped my spirits and may have helped me to get well.

My First Real Great Sorrow

In December of that year, illness struck again. All six members of the family were in bed at the same time with influenza. With high fever and near death, my parents took care of us four boys. Little Edwin developed pneumonia and died on his second birthday, December 18. Dad had already bought two tricycles for him and Jimmy for Christmas. Jimmy was nearly four years old. Of course, Dad had to send one tricycle back. We were all up for the funeral but still very weak.

But for their faith in Jesus Christ, I do not see how my parents could have stood the grief. The red clay graveyard was filled with the graves of friends, some victims of the war and some victims of the epidemic. When they lowered the little casket containing our little Edwin into the ground, it was raining so hard that the midgets were dancing in the red mud. This certainly did not prepare us for a very happy Christmas. But Dad and Mother did all they could to cheer up the boys.

Our Clubhouse

We boys read a great deal. We read the Rover Boys series, the Swift Brothers series, and Edgar Rice Burrows' and Zane Grey's novels. Our parents bought for us the Junior Classics and all of Kipling's works. We read most of those books underground by candlelight. We dug a hole in the ground about eight cubic feet in dimension, covered it over with boards, and piled dirt on top of the boards. Then we sank a shaft about three feet by four feet, eight feet deep, and about twelve feet away, and tunneled to that underground clubhouse. Joe Tom Nuckle's people had an indoor bathroom put in their house; so they let us have the superstructure of their old outdoor relic. We knocked out the two-hole seat, erected the building over the shaft, and put a ladder down to the tunnel. This was the entrance to our subterranean clubhouse. We placed a padlock on the door to vouchsafe privacy.

"Iron-Cord" Tonic

When I was nine years old, I decided it was time for me to take up smoking. Taking my five pennies, I went down to "Hamburger Jack's" diner and bought three cigarettes and two cheroots. I had heard that Jack broke packs to sell them individually to little boys.

I went home and hid in the smokehouse where we had bacon, hams, and link sausages being slowly smoked. I smoked a cigarette and a cheroot; then I went into the house and brushed my teeth and gargled with Listerine.

That night I was to go to a Sunday school party at my mother's church. I left home early, and my mother saw me slip some wood stick matches out of the kitchen and stop by the smokehouse to pick up the cigarettes and the cheroot I had stashed out there. I went on to the church where I had an engagement to meet two of my pals. I gave each of them a cigarette and a match, and I was lighting my cheroot when I heard my buddies scamper around the church. I was seated on a big concrete church step with a lighted match between my eyes and whatever or whoever scared my friends. I shook out the light and looked up to see my mother standing there. She asked, "What are you doing, son?" I said, "I am lighting Jesse Oliver's cheroot." She said,

"Come on home. I am going to light your cheroot." She kept that promise.

Mother used to complain to my father that there were no hickory trees in West Texas, but she found a likely substitute for a hickory switch. She folded an electric iron cord neatly and gave me a dose of iron-cord tonic that completely took away from me the desire to smoke. I promised Mother that if she would quit whipping me I would not smoke until I was twenty-one years old. I kept that promise; and since I was converted when I was nineteen, I never did start smoking. It was not difficult because I was engaged in athletics all through my youth, and training rules forbade smoking anyhow. I thanked my mother many times for that iron-cord remedy for smoking, and I recommend it to parents everywhere.

My Tenth Birthday

On my tenth birthday my parents asked me what I wanted for a birthday present. My request was a quart of buttermilk. Mother gave me a nickel to pay for it and sent me up to Mr. Highliker's to get it. Mr. Highliker had some apricot trees with limbs extending over his back fence and over the public sidewalk. Fruit was ripe, and those apricots looked so good that I reasoned that since they were hanging in public domain I had a right to take some of them. I ate five. But by the time I got home, my conscience was hurting so badly that I threw up those delicious apricots. Mother baked some cornbread for me to have with my buttermilk, and I had a happy birthday despite my smarting conscience.

Junior Boy Scout

Now that I was ten years old, I was eligible to become a junior Boy Scout. Rev. Mr. Judd, the Presbyterian minister, was the scoutmaster in Chillicothe. He built a gymnasium-scout hall behind the Presbyterian church. There we wrestled and boxed and exercised with dumbbells and barbells and other equipment and learned to "do our best" to keep ourselves "physically fit, mentally awake, and morally straight."

Fred Stucky was a splendid young man who was becoming an Eagle Scout. He was kind to us younger boys. I played on the baseball team with him and the older boys. Fred knew a lot of science, especially physics. He turned a shed in his back yard into a laboratory and built a crystal-set, wireless receiver. We used to spend hours there experimenting with old telephone batteries, ringing bells and buzzers, and getting little electric shocks. We had a wonderful time listening to the "wireless machine" with "squawks, dits, dots, wheezes, and whirs" coming from forty miles away.

The first wireless, or radio, that I ever heard was on the Chillicothe High School campus. They built there a little one-room house with an antenna strung between two poles and grounded with a wire fastened to the handle of a zinc tub and buried deep. Most of the people of the town went single file in and out of the house to listen to a lot of static and very little broadcasting. I remember that one night they phoned long distance to Childress, forty miles away, and asked the operator to go on the air. He played a Victrola for us, playing the same records over and over. He played "The Yellow Dog Blues" and "The Preacher and the Bear." The static supplied extra sound effects like the bear growling.

Airplane! Airplane!

Every time an airplane landed in some field near Chillicothe, it caused a lot of excitement. All of the people except the bedridden and the very infirm went to see it. They raced across fields in buggies, wagons, and cars, on horses, bicycles, and motorcycles, and hundreds afoot, yelling as they ran, "Airplane! Airplane! Airplane!" The pilot sitting in the cockpit, wearing a trench coat, goggles, and an aviator cap buckled under his chin, was a keen-looking specimen of Homo sapiens.

Lew began working in Griffin's Drugstore when he was only ten years old. He was a "soda jerker" and a front-end clerk. Later he became a pharmacist.

One very cold night Fred Stucky and Lew and I camped out at Wanders Creek. We gathered wood all along the banks of the creek and built a fire. After we cooked our supper, as we sat around the fire eating, Lew pointed at a knot in a little log he had carried on his shoulder about seventy-five yards. With his finger close to the knothole out of which smoke was curling, he said, "Look at that smooooooke!" At that moment a rattlesnake stuck his forked tongue through, followed by his head, and then came crawling out. Lew jumped back and stepped on the edge of a big iron skillet of hot grease, turning it up and splashing the scalding grease on his ankle. Of course, we killed the snake.

Early in the morning we broke the ice on the creek and went swimming.

CHAPTER V

Early High School Years

W hen I was thirteen I entered high school and played football on the freshmen team of Chillicothe High School, the Chillicothe Freshmen Longhorns. I got to play the entire game against Quanah High School Freshmen.

Return to Alabama

We moved back to Alabama in November of that year. The rest of the family preceded my father several weeks as he stayed in Texas to sell our house and take care of the business. We stayed temporarily on my grandfather's farm, a mile from Thomasville High School. My father arrived for Christmas, and we had a happy reunion. Then we rented a house and moved into town. Dad bought out the American Cafe and operated it for nearly two years.

Life in Thomasville

Uncle Frank gave me a job cleaning the soda fountain in his drugstore every morning before school. I had to get up at five o'clock every morning to perform this chore because I then cleaned the Farmers and Merchants Bank before going to school. For cleaning the soda fountain, I received ten cents a day; and for cleaning the bank, I received $1.25 a week. At the end of each month, I helped to get out the bank statements. My job was to seal the envelopes and stick on the stamps. For this I received $3.00. I used to say, "I am a draft clerk. I open the windows to let in the draft. And I am a stockholder. I hold the farmer's stock while they bank."

Each morning at ten o'clock I had a vacant hour in my schedule at school; so I was permitted to meet the northbound morning train to get the *Mobile Register* and deliver it to about twenty customers. In the evening I delivered the *Birmingham News*.

Most afternoons when school was out, I hurried home to parch peanuts and sell them for five cents a bag. I filled a market basket with sacks of peanuts and sold a few bags on the streets and in the stores while on my way to the "header" mill—a mill where they made barrel heads. There I could always sell out. I usually finished the task at about 4:30 P.M. and had time to do a little homework at my daddy's restaurant before time to help out with the supper rush. I would then meet the southbound evening train to get and deliver the *Birmingham News*.

I followed this crowded schedule every day except during football and baseball seasons in addition to making deliveries sometimes for the drugstore, for which I received tips.

High School Football

When I was a sophomore at fourteen years of age, I weighed only 135 pounds. I went out for football; but the manager, the student keeper of the equipment, Leon Dunning, told me I was too little to play football and refused to issue a uniform to me. I told him that I had played with the Chillicothe Freshmen Longhorns, but he was not impressed. Rejected, dejected, and almost in tears, I went down on the field just to watch and wish. Coach Tom Borham told the boys not to catch a punt like a forward pass but to let it come into the stomach and trap it there with both arms. He then sent the backfield men down the gridiron to catch punts. I started home, but I looked around, and a stray punt was coming off field toward me. I caught it just right. The coach called and asked me why I was not out for football. I told him, and he said, "Go tell Leon Dunning that I said to give you a uniform."

Coach put me at right end on the second team, and I got to play in several games that year toward the ends of the games. Our first trip was to Selma. We were told to be at the high school not later than eight o'clock Saturday morning. I got there on time, but the team had left for Selma. I was about the most disappointed teenager in the world; but as I started across the campus to go home and tell my folks that I got left, I saw the Andersons' Buick coming. There were Dovie Fair Anderson, Jr., Joe Anderson, their mother, and Coach Borham coming to pick me up. I felt very important.

If one could feel so bad as I felt over thinking I had missed that trip, how infinitely worse it will be for one to realize he has missed Heaven for all eternity.

Coach Tom Borham

Coach Borham was a real hero to me. He taught us to play hard but to play fairly. He was strict on training rules. He drilled us over and over on technical fundamentals of football. He did not return to Thomasville in the fall of 1924. Mr. Fred White was our coach that year. I liked him very much, too.

I did not hear from Coach Borham for thirty-three years. In 1956 I was holding a revival campaign in the First Baptist Church of Ozark, Alabama. We had morning and evening services. On Monday morning a lovely lady came to me and said, "I am Mrs. Borham. I am a Methodist, and our pastor, Rev. Charles Lidell, had to be out of town this week but told us that he was converted under your ministry in 1932 at Butler, Alabama. He wanted the Methodist people to attend your meetings and to be sure to give you his greetings."

I said, "I remember Charles Lidell. He attended our meetings every night with his mother, who was the postmistress in Butler. Give him my regards. You said your name was Mrs. Borham?

My first football coach was named Tom Borham."

She said, "My husband's name is Tom. He used to coach football."

It turned out that Coach Tom Borham had been a colonel in the army during World War II and was the judge of Ozark. Mrs. Borham went home and told her husband about our conversation, and he attended our meetings regularly. The Borhams invited me to their lovely home for tea on Saturday afternoon. Judge Borham and I went into their beautiful flower garden, and I said, "Judge Borham, I want to thank you for what you meant to me when I was a fourteen-year-old boy. You taught me the importance of the fundamentals of football, and that must have had a lot to do with my concept of the fundamentals of the Christian Faith."

He said, "Monroe, I have been thinking of those days as I have listened to you preach, and I have thought that I wish I could go back to those days and put into my influence what you have been preaching."

I asked, "Judge, are you saved?"

He answered, "No. According to what you have been preaching, I cannot say that I am. I am a Methodist steward, and I try to live a good life, but I have not been born again."

I urged him to settle it there in the garden, but he wanted to think about it. It was one of the biggest thrills of my life when Judge Tom Borham, my old coach, came down the aisle the next night to settle the matter. He accepted Jesus Christ as his Saviour and joined the First Baptist Church of Ozark.

City of Selma

Although I had been to Mobile several times and had been to New Orleans, Shreveport, Fort Worth, and Dallas, that football trip to the little city of Selma was to me, a fourteen-year-old boy from Thomasville with its population of 1002, a thrilling experience. Aside from the ecstasy of playing a few minutes on a varsity high school football team, we walked down the sidewalk of the main street of that tremendous metropolis of nearly twenty thousand people, with the "clang, clang" of public carriages and the "clip, clop" of the horses' hooves, and the "wugah" of automobile horns in that day before horn tooting except for emergency was outlawed. I saw a bowl of wax fruit in the window of Woolworth's and felt that I had seen the ultimate in human ingenuity.

In my junior year in high school, I played right end on the first team; but halfway through the season, I was laid aside by a student's long-bladed pocketknife.

Long Pants

It was customary for boys to wear knee-length pants and long black-ribbed stockings until they were fifteen or sixteen years old. When I was a little boy, I used to wear holes in my stockings at the knees as well as in my right thumbnail playing marbles. I was always breaking the buttons off the knee straps of my knickers, and I would use safety pins, which would soon tear holes in the straps. I also hated to wear garters to hold up my stockings. So aside from the fact that long pants were a mark of maturity, I was very glad when I was allowed to wear long pants.

The power plant in Thomasville closed down every night at eleven o'clock, and there was no electricity until six the next morning. That was before the time of electric refrigerators and clocks. Ice was delivered in trucks, and various size blocks were chiseled from huge three-hundred-pound blocks and delivered to domestic ice boxes. When the ice man left his truck for his task, it was often raided by little children getting ice chips.

At exactly ten minutes before eleven each night, the lights would wink three times. This signified that they would go out altogether in ten minutes. It was also a signal for me to head for home, for eleven o'clock was the deadline for me to be home.

One night a few nights after I put on long pants, I stayed out until 11:30. When I got home, I went into my parents' bedroom to get an oil lamp. They had gone to bed but were not asleep. Dad said, "Monroe, it is 11:30."

I answered, "I wear long pants and I guess I am big enough to know when to come home."

Dad was on the other side of the bed from where I stood. It will always be a mystery to me how he got out from under the cover and over my mother so quickly; but when I finally got up off the floor, I understood that I had a lot of growing up to do.

The changing to long pants was a big event in the life of a boy. He was spanked by the other long-pants wearers the first time he wore his long pants to school. They called this "getting his fresh pork." They certainly got mine. Some of them were butchers. When Si Nichols got my fresh pork, he used a board that looked like a bed slat and swatted me with all of his might— and he was a big fellow.

Stabbed With a Knife

When Isaac Harrison came to school in long pants, he said he was not going to take that hazing. The boys gathered around him to reason with him and were encouraging him to be a good sport and take his spanking. Suddenly Arvil Phylan gave him a tap with a little stick and ran away. Isaac turned around and came at me. I threw up my left arm to fend off his blow, but he had a knife in his hand. The blade stuck all the way up into my forearm to the elbow. I knocked him down with my right fist. He reached up from the ground and stabbed toward my heart. I was looking at the gash on my left arm. I dropped my arm to protect my heart, striking his hand, and his knife stuck deep into my left side. I ran eight blocks to Dr. Kimbrough's office. When I got there, my socks were completely wet with blood, as were most of my clothes. Dr. Kimbrough packed my arm and my side with gauze dipped in tincture of iodine, and a friend drove me in the back seat of a Ford car over rough dirt and gravel roads sixty-five miles to the hospital in Selma, where I spent fourteen days. Dr. Harper, the surgeon who sewed me

Monroe, age 16. (1925)

up, said that if the cut had been on the right side, he could have taken out my appendix. He said that if the knife blade had gone a quarter of an inch farther in either direction, it would have got a main artery and would have killed me. "Are they not all ministering spirits, sent forth to minister for them who shall be heirs of salvation?" (Heb. 1:14).

My mother was a piano teacher. During the three weeks following my stay in the hospital, I took piano lessons from her; but when I was able to get out of the house, I dropped piano lessons.

CHAPTER VI

Move to Birmingham

We moved to Birmingham in March, 1925. Uncle Will Moseley was the owner and manager of the Imperial Candy Company, a wholesale candy factory on First Avenue in Birmingham. He went into the business of buying bankrupt concerns and running bankrupt sales. He got my father to join him. They would go to court and bid on bankrupt stock. The bid was never over twenty percent of the wholesale value of the goods. They would slash the retail prices and run a sale at the site where the store had operated, then move the leftover odds and ends to Pratt City in Suburban Birmingham, where we had a large two-story building. The top story of this building we used for a warehouse and the main floor for a general mercantile establishment called "Everybody's Store."

One of the first bankrupt concerns they bought was a coffin factory. Then they bought some dry goods stores—Jacob's Clothing Store on First Avenue in Birmingham, Phelps' Dry Goods and Clothing Store on 26th Street, a creamery in Fairfield, a T-model Ford Bender Brace Factory, a grocery store at Mulga, a jewelry store, and many other businesses.

No wonder they called the Pratt City store "Everybody's Store."

We moved to Pratt City to run Everybody's Store and bankrupt sales throughout Greater Birmingham.

Ensley High School

I went to Ensley High School my last three semesters in high school, graduating in June 1926. Here I was in the Reserve Officers Training Corps. Every Friday we had inspection. We had to have our guns (World War I Springfield rifles weighing sixteen pounds) shining like new, our uniforms clean and pressed, and our woolen leghorns neatly wrapped. That was sheer punishment for me as wool next to my skin causes it to itch. But it was good discipline for me.

Ensley was a splendid high school. They won the state championship in football in 1924, and in 1925 we were beaten only once.

My high school courses at Thomasville and Ensley included Latin, English Literature, American Literature, Civics, Biology, Chemistry, Physics, two years of Algebra, Plane Geometry, and History, four years of football, track, two years of baseball, R.O.T.C, Expression, and Music Appreciation. Despite the fact that I was kept very busy, I was very worldly. I began to drink and attend dances before I was fifteen years old in Thomasville and continued these practices in Birmingham.

A Job in the T.C.I. Commissary

The day after I graduated from high school, Mr. Percy James, a steward in my mother's church, saw me on a street car. I was on my way to look for a job in downtown Birmingham. Mr. James asked, "Monroe, now that you are out of high school, what are you planning to do?" I answered, "I expect to attend Birmingham Southern College in the fall to study pre-med; but right now I am going to town to look for a job." He said, "If you will come by my office in the Tennessee Coal, Iron, and Railroad Company Commissary at Pratt City tomorrow morning, I think I can help you get a job."

I went to work the next day, substituting for one of the clerks who was on vacation. I substituted for a different clerk for every fortnight throughout the summer. I got experience working in the snackshop, the meat market, the grocery department, the warehouse, and feed store. I unloaded boxcars of hundred-pound sacks of feed and toned up my muscles for football.

CHAPTER VII

A Shameful Record

E xcept during football season, I worked each Saturday in the Commissary during the school year and then throughout a second summer.

My dear parents paid my tuition at Birmingham Southern College, and I squandered most of the money I made. I went on in my worldly ways and helped make the twenties roar.

My First Car

In 1927 I bought for $25.00 a 1923 T-model Ford which was in perfect condition. The only thing wrong with it was that it did not have a top on it. This was easily remedied. I bought a mammoth yellow umbrella which I raised in time of rain.

Bill, Joe, and Frank Lacey, each the first cousin of the other two, were pals of mine. Bill's brother-in-law, Earl Penny, was the head motorcycle mechanic for the City of Birmingham. He obtained for Bill a famous Harley-Davidson motorcycle known to all the cops as "Old Rags." Bill traded me half interest in "Old Rags" for half interest in "Odney-Hassen," my T-model Ford. I will not explain why the jalopy bore such a strange appellation except to say that everyone named his car in that era. Bill got his brother-in-law to have Odney-Hassen painted in the city shop a Rolls Royce blue with fire-truck red wheels. When I put on my yellow rain slicker, autographed by a hundred students, and raised my bright yellow umbrella and drove

Odney-Hassen across the campus, even the guys in raccoon coats driving Stutz Bearcats gave a second look, although I never knew whether it was a look of envy or a look of disgust.

Bill Lacey and I alternated in keeping Odney-Hassen while the other one had Old Rags, and vice versa. I rode Rags one day at ninety-six miles an hour, and the road in front of me looked like a funnel.

Helping Make the Twenties Roar

During these years of frolicking, drinking, dancing, and running around with a wild gang, I had no peace; and there was an insatiable hunger in my soul for something better.

I could not stay out of a fight. I was very strong. I could lift 1400 pounds one inch from the floor and could move 1400 pounds one inch with a punch from the shoulder. I wrestled and boxed and knew how to use my "dukes." I tried not to be a bully; but if anyone made what I considered a derogatory remark about me, my friends, or anyone I happened to like, I felt that it was my duty to make him retract his statement or fight.

Before I was saved, extracurricular activities took precedence with me over academic matters.

A regular war between Birmingham Southern College, a Methodist school located on the western side of Birmingham, and Howard College, a Southern Baptist school located on the eastern side of the city, broke out each year about two or three weeks before the annual football game.

My first semester at Birmingham Southern in the fall of 1926, the war began when Howard students invaded the Southern campus in the middle of the night and defaced several buildings with bold, profane lettering done in the Howard colors, crimson and blue. Birmingham Southern students coming in late at night discovered this vandalism and retaliated by going to Howard and painting on their buildings with black and gold paint. This was followed by Howard students breaking into the Science Hall at Birmingham Southern to steal a mounted panther, symbol of the Birmingham Southern football team. They phoned the men's dormitory to tell the Southern men that if they would come to the Howard campus, they could have their panther. However, when they appeared on the Howard campus in the football equipment truck, they were ambushed. A barrage of stones and bricks greeted them, striking two students on their heads and requiring hospitalization.

It was in the fall of 1927 that I was attacked in front of the Temple Theater by two Howard students, a sophomore by the name of Billy McDonald and a freshman named Gaye. I threw McDonald on the curb and knocked Gaye down on the sidewalk. Then a big crowd of Howard students poured out of the theater. One of the students had seen us mixing it up and had run into the theater to tell a whole gang of Howard students.

Kidnapped

They piled all over me, ripped my brand-new overcoat to shreds, tied my hands behind me, got me in the back seat of a car, and drove me to the Pi.K.A. house on the Howard campus. On the seven-mile drive to Howard, freshman Gaye beat me in the mouth, so that my lips were cut by my teeth, and tried to get me to say, "Yea, Howard!" This I refused to do.

They took me to the above-mentioned fraternity house in that professedly Christian school amid language analogous to the profanity on the Watergate tapes. With my hands tied behind me, I had my head shaved with a straight razor. When they had me looking like Kojack, and with several gashes on my head, they sicked their bulldog on me and let him get to the end of his chain a few inches from my face. After this they painted my head with oil paint, half of it red and half of it blue. Then they moved me to the top floor of the men's dormitory, where the freshmen were ordered to guard me through the night. Lest I break out the window and swing down and drop to the ground, they took every stitch of my clothing.

Dovey Fair Anderson from Thomasville was an upperclassman

at Howard and lived in the dormitory. He persuaded them to
let him bring me a towel with one end dipped in kerosene to
wash the paint off my head. He was afraid those razor nicks on
my head would get infected. I cleaned my head and then washed
the kerosene out of the towel and used it for a wet sarong.

War on Campus

Many Birmingham Southern men, having heard that they had
me at Howard, made a valiant though futile effort to rescue me.
They came out en masse and fought on the Howard campus until a riot squad was called out to break it up. One upperclassman
with a broken nose came into the room where I was being held
and said that several men on both sides were hurt.

The next morning they brought my ragged clothes and told
me to dress for breakfast. They took me to the campus dining
room, where the girls as well as the men could see my Kojack-
type head and laugh at me. Then they announced that Birmingham Southern students had caught one of their star football players, and they had agreed to turn us loose at 11:00 A.M.

I Get a Nickname

When I got back to Birmingham Southern with my shaved
head, I screwed up my mouth and did some monkey antics. I
was already called "Mon" Parker; so when someone shouted,
"Monk" Parker, the nickname stuck. I thought I would get rid
of that nickname the next year, having been converted and having transferred to Bob Jones College. But I walked into the lob-
by of the men's dormitory which was filled with students, and
there sat a transfer student from Birmingham Southern. Upon
seeing me, he jumped up and shouted, "Monk Parker, what are
you doing here?"

He told the students about my monkey act; and before long,
they had coaxed me into doing it. So the nickname stayed with
me until after I had finished college, had spent nearly six years

The Birmingham P

NO. 260   TWO SECTIONS (Section One)   BIRMINGHAM, ALABAMA, FRIDAY, NOVEMBER 18, 1927

STRUGGLE IS HINTED IN DE

Students Stage Free-For-All Fight
25,000 To Witness Dedication Game

Bloody Noses in Evidence At Local Colleges After Battle

HOLDING HOSTAGES

Four Howard, One Southern Boys Lose "Scalps"

A FREE-FOR-ALL FIGHT at First av. and 21st st., and hair-clippings for four Howard students and one Birmingham-Southern student were the highlights of an active night in the feud between the two local colleges today.

Police broke up the free-for-all after a few bloody noses and wrenched thumbs had been exchanged in the most collegiate manner. There were at least 100 boys in the downtown battle.

In addition, each of the schools is holding a student of its competitor as a "hostage."

Howard students are holding Monroe Parker, Birmingham-Southern sophomore, and Birmingham-Southern students are holding Frank Hollifield, Howard freshman. Heads of both hostages had already been clipped.

Other Howard students to lose their scalps in the feud were Jimmy Shelburne, chairman of the Howard parade committee and a member of the group which stole the Birmingham-Southern Panther last year; Richard Shaffer and Leonard Allen.

Shaffer and Allen were captured in front of Loew's Temple theater, where the two colleges held a joint pop meeting last night, and Shelburne was taken at Simpson High school, a short distance from the Birmingham-Southern campus.

Birmingham-Southern students made a raid on the Howard campus in great strength shortly after midnight, searching for the stone scheduled to have been placed on the campus in memory of the theft of the Panther last year, but found that the monument had not arrived.

16,000 Tickets Already Sold For Big Contest

LEGION HEAD HERE

Other Distinguished Men Will Arrive By To-morrow

WITH United States senators, governors, the national commander of the American Legion and other notables present, 25,000 people were expected to be at Legion Field stadium Saturday for the dedication game between Birmingham-Southern and Howard colleges.

This will be the biggest crowd ever gathered to see a football game in Birmingham. More than 16,000 tickets have already been sold.

Gates of the municipal stadium will be thrown open at 12:30 p.m. and the referee's whistle will start the game promptly at 2.

Ticket sales took an added spurt Friday, following announcment of a junior chamber of commerce committee that permission from big department store owners that as many employes as possible would be allowed a half holiday to attend the game, provided the employe had purchased a ticket at the time he applies for permission of leave.

The committee visited most of the larger stores and merchants fell in line with the proposition, holding the only condition that their business not be interfered with too seriously.

One merchant, who asked that his name be withheld, bought 20 choice seats to be distributed to disabled World War veterans and Gold Star mothers. These tickets can be had at the American Legion office.

Edward Spafford, national commander of the legion, was the first distinguished guest to arrive. He arrived at 8 a.m. today at the official headquarters in the Bankhead hotel.

in full-time evangelistic work, and then returned to Bob Jones College to serve as Director of Religious Activities.

I was only seventeen when I started to Birmingham Southern College and was not mature enough to handle the extremely heavy load I allowed a sophomore girl in the registrar's office to pile on me. I don't blame her because she told me that I could not take a pre-med course and play football. I insisted on playing football. She signed me up for the following courses:

Biology	-	4 semester hours
Chemistry	-	4 semester hours
History	-	3 semester hours
French	-	3 semester hours
Algebra	-	3 semester hours
English	-	3 semester hours
Football	-	½ semester hour

These classes occupied all the morning class periods Monday through Friday except two. Football filled the afternoons till dark. Afterwards I showered and took the better part of an hour to get home. Then I had to frolic, as my father called it. Picture shows, dances, dates, and the like took several evenings a week. Drawings for biology, homework for algebra, learning vocabularies for French, studying for chemistry and other classes had to go begging. I not only lacked maturation but also lacked motivation until I was saved. So I made a poor academic record. I did better after I was saved, and I finished college with a high "B" average, doing still better in my graduate work.

CHAPTER VIII

Conversion

I joined the Baptist church in Edgewood, Texas, when I was eight years old, but I was not converted. I knew many of the truths of the Bible. I knew about Jesus, His wonderful life, teachings, and miracles, His crucifixion and His resurrection, and I gave intellectual assent to all of the Christian teachings. But I was a sinner and knew it. When my brother Lew joined the church, I also wanted to join; so I followed him down the aisle.

A well-meaning deacon sat down by my side and asked if I came by "profession of faith." To me, an eight-year-old boy, that word "profession" had something to do with being a doctor or a dentist or a schoolteacher perhaps; so I asked him, "What, sir?"

He asked, "Do you want to be baptized?" But he failed to lead me to Jesus Christ. Since I knew that baptism was in the offing when I joined the church, I answered, "Yes, sir."

The deacon said, "Pastor, Monroe Parker comes by profession of faith." Another well-meaning deacon said, "I make a motion we receive him." Another seconded the motion. The pastor said, "All in favor, let it be known by saying, 'Aye.' Any opposed, let it be known by saying, 'Nay.'" There were no nays.

That afternoon I was baptized with several others in Edgewood Lake. Several of us tarried in the bathhouse till the crowd left and then went swimming. Swimming on Sunday was taboo according to general standards of Christian people in that day and according to my conscience. It still is taboo according to my conscience. But I violated my conscience as soon as I was baptized. When I got home, my dear Christian mother said, "Now, Son, you are a church member, and the Devil is going to be after you." I did not tell her that he already had me although I knew that he did.

I was afraid to go after the cow that evening. I walked backwards down through the pasture so that in case the Devil jumped out from behind a stump I would be ready to run without having to turn around.

I went on to church and Sunday school and Baptist Young People's Union; but I was a Hell-bound sinner, and I knew it.

Unsaved Church Member

For eleven years I was an unsaved church member. I was a worldly college student, rebellious against authority of any kind. I thought I was angry with the establishment but was angry with myself because I had failed to live up to the ideals that had been held up for me all through my youth.

Mother and Dad often attended each other's church although Dad was a Baptist and Mother was a Methodist. The Methodist Episcopal Church, South, in my youth believed in individual salvation and was much more orthodox than the M. E. Church with which it and the Methodist Protestant Church later merged.

Although I joined a Baptist church when I was eight years of age, I used to alternate between the Methodist and Baptist churches. Since I had to go to church often, I chose to go to Mother's church because although I was not a born-again Christian, I enjoyed the big pipe organ in the Chillicothe Methodist Church and the grand old hymns they sang: "Jesus, Lover of My Soul," "Rock of Ages," "The Old Rugged Cross," "O for a Thousand Tongues," "Fairest Lord Jesus," and "The Gloria Patri."

I also enjoyed the spirited singing in the Baptist church with such songs as "He Included Me," "When the Roll Is Called Up

Yonder," "Whosoever Meaneth Me," "His Promise to Me," "Let the Lower Lights Be Burning," and my father's favorite song, "How Tedious and Tasteless the Hours."

When I was ten years old, I became embittered and skeptical about the piety of one of the deacons of the Baptist church. I was promised ten dollars to chop the weeds and clear a large field next to the church. I worked hard. The ground was like dusty, red cement, but the tough weeds were very prolific and were up to my shoulders over most of the field. It took several weeks to clear the area with the light hoe I was using. I had to stop every few minutes to file my hoe.

When the job was finished and I went to receive my pay from the deacon who hired me, he said, "The Southern Baptist Convention has a campaign to raise $75,000,000.00, and our church has been assessed a certain amount; so we will assess you the amount of that work." Every time that deacon led in prayer, I thought of what Jesus said about making long prayers for a pretense.

I am sure he was a good man, and my attitude was wrong; but I got some boys to help turn over his outdoor toilet on Halloween night. We hid in the alley until he was in it before we upset it.

I finally stopped going to church except when my parents insisted on it.

One Saturday night I came home drunk. My parents were so heartbroken that they knelt by my bed and prayed for their worldly, lost son. The next morning I volunteered to go to the Methodist Sunday school with my mother.

Unsaved Sunday School Teacher

When I got to the church, the Sunday school superintendent asked me to teach a class. I said, "I am not a Christian."

"Oh," he said, "aren't you a church member?"

I answered, "I am a Baptist."

In the years since that day, I have concluded that if we could get half the church members saved, we would see a great revival. In fact, I think if we could get half of the preachers in America converted, we would see a mighty revival that would stop the floodtide of evil and turn America back to God. Just belonging to a church did not save me.

The superintendent went on, "I know you have not studied the lesson; so just go down and read the quarterly to the boys. They are just juniors."

That man was a good man, and he meant well; and I believe God led him to enlist me, for it led to my conversion. But I do not advocate putting an unsaved sinner in charge of a Sunday school class of any age people, especially ten-year-old boys.

The juniors need the best teacher in the church. But I went down to the Junior Department and taught a class of ten-year-old boys. They begged me to take their class regularly, not because I was fit to be a Sunday school teacher but because I was an athlete and they thought it would be great to have me teach their class.

I said, "All right, boys, I will teach the class." But I said to myself, "I've got to be a Christian. I've got to live a Christian life." But I did not have life. How could I live a life I did not have?

I made good resolutions. I resolved to quit drinking. I was not a drunkard. I could take a drink or leave it alone., The fellow who says he can do that usually takes it. I said, "I will quit cursing." I never had the habit of taking God's name in vain, and I don't deserve any credit for that. When I was a little boy, I heard an old man say, "If you could use your own air to curse God, it would not be quite so bad; but when you have to breathe the air God gives you to take His name in vain, that is the depth of ingratitude." Well, I always had a contempt for an ingrate; so I made up my mind that I would not take God's name in vain. And now that I was going to try to be a Christian, I resolved to quit cursing.

I said, "I will quit gambling." I had never been to Las Vegas to play the one-armed bandits or the roulette wheels, but I used to bet on the ball games. That is just as much gambling as spending a fortune at the races. It is just as much gambling to match for a Coca Cola as it is to shoot craps all day and play poker all night. I did shoot craps and play poker occasionally, but I quit it all.

Reformation Did Not Save

I catalogued all of my sins and resolved to quit them, and I kept my resolutions very well; but I was not saved. I knew it, and my father knew it. One Sunday after we had come home from church while we were waiting for dinner, he reached over and took from my hand a little black book in which I had phone numbers and addresses of friends. He said, "Mon, let me write something in your book." He wrote on the flyleaf, "Be not deceived; God is not mocked: for whatsoever a man soweth, that shall he also reap" (Gal. 6:7). That afternoon I went to hear Dr. Bob Shuler preach. He took from his pocket a little black notebook that looked like the one I had in my pocket, in which my father had written the Scripture verse, and read that same text. I felt to see if he had my notebook. I felt like the man Amos wrote about, "As if a man did flee from a lion, and a bear met him; or went into the house, and leaned his hand on the wall, and a serpent bit him" (Amos 5:19).

One thing Dr. Shuler said stuck with me. He screamed out in a high-pitched voice, "Your sins crucified Jesus!" All through that week those words rang in my memory. They echoed a thousand times.

The next Sunday morning the lesson was on the stoning of Stephen. When Stephen was dying, he lifted up his eyes and saw Jesus standing at the right hand of the Father in Heaven, and he cried with a loud voice, "Lord, lay not this sin to their charge" (Acts 7:60).

I said, "You see, boys, Stephen had the spirit of Jesus. He prayed for those who put Him to death." This pricked my conscience. One of my greatest sins was hating those who wronged me.

"Your Sins Crucified Jesus"

Then Dr. Shuler's words came to me, and I said, "Boys, your sins crucified Jesus." The boys hung their heads in shame, and I said, "My sins crucified Jesus. I am a sinner, and I have never been saved. Pray for me." The boys bowed their heads and began to pray, and I bowed my head and trusted Jesus Christ as my personal Saviour. At that moment I was born again.

In the church service that followed, I went forward to tell the pastor, Brother R. L. Baker, and joined the Methodist Episcopal Church, South. This was my mother's church. I needed indoctrination, which I received beginning that fall.

I Met Bob Jones

How wonderfully God leads in the life of His child. Thursday night after I was saved on Sunday morning, Dr. Bob Jones came to our little church and gave his famous sermon-lecture on "The Perils of America." He told about the college which he had founded and which was one year old.

Dr. Jones usually preached to great crowds, but on this occasion there was a very small crowd. The service had not been properly announced and promoted. I know that God sent him to Pratt City to contact me.

CHAPTER IX

Call to Preach

In September 1928 I transferred to Bob Jones College, which was located for its first six years on beautiful St. Andrews Bay near Panama City, Florida. I was very happy there with young people who saw life as I had come to see it and with wonderful Christian teachers. The college was located on a circle one mile around and nearly a mile from the bay, and the property between the campus and the bay was owned by the college. Bayous on either side of this area formed the college property into a peninsula. We enjoyed swimming in one of the bayous and in the bay. The bayou was deep, and we could dive there. We also had a high-diving tower in the bay. The men and women alternated in the use of the bayou and the bay. We boys sometimes enjoyed nocturnal swims. If sharks came into the bay at night, as they sometimes did, we could usually see them outlined in the phosphorescent water.

My years in Bob Jones College happen to have been the only years the college played interscholastic football.

In 1928

Coach Allison moved me from right end to right tackle and then to fullback. In those days football players played both offense and defense. My junior year I was alternate captain with John Parks Tyson, captain. I played quarterback on offense and backed up the line on defense. Tyson played right end. He could change speed better than any pass receiver I ever saw and was great at catching touchdown passes.

I punted, passed, and ran with the ball. I was elected captain my senior year. We had a good season. Since we were not in an association, there were not many small colleges we could schedule, although there were some. We played a number of high schools and allowed them to use alumni.

We ran over Carabell 73 to 0 and Apalachicola 70 to 0. However, Palmer College tied us, and Troy State Normal College beat us 12 to 0. That was our last game and our only defeat in four years.

In that game I was tremendously handicapped. I had my left ankle fractured in practice the week before, but we taped it well and Coach Crumpton put me in the game to call signals from the position of right guard. I played sixty minutes with terrific pain in my ankle. Fred Brown was right tackle. We agreed, "Let's not let them gain an inch on our side of the line." They did not. Fred was good not only on defense but also on offense, and he made some great avenues for the ball carrier to travel.

While we played hard to win our games, we tried just as hard to leave a good testimony with our opponents.

Two years after we played Carabell, Jimmy Mercer was converted and said he was called to preach. His brother, who had been saved a short time, said, "Go to Bob Jones College. I played against Bob Jones with Carabell. Those were the best men I ever saw. They would knock us down and then help us up and say, 'God bless you, Buddy.' We would take God's name in vain, and they would say, 'We will pray for you, friend.' " So Jimmy went to Bob Jones College and became Dr. James Mercer, the evangelist.

Originally at Bob Jones College the Bible Conferences were held between semesters. My first year we had eight speakers each day; and though we got weary and some students had to take sofa pillows to the chapel to sit on, we loved every minute of it. That year we heard Dr. Melvin Grove Kyle, the famous archeologist and editor of the great five-volume work,

MONROE PARKER—Fullback
"Monk"

"Monk,' Alternate Captain, was the strong man on the team, and was always ready to place his driving power either on the line or in the backfield. "Monk" always showed his strength and driving power in the line plunges.

MONROE PARKER—Captain—Quarterback
Monk displayed rare judgment in his direction of the Swamper's attack and was a line ripper of the old school.

From college yearbook. (1931)

International Standard Bible Encyclopedia; Dr. Whaylon, a New Jersey pastor; Dr. Orr, from Xenia Theological Seminary, who preached on Heaven and then went to Heaven the following week; Dr. Rousseau, a colorful Florida pastor who fought in the Boer War; Dr. J. B. Culpepper, a great old evangelist who was an octogenarian and could preach the stars down; and Dr. L. W. Munhall, who was ninety-two years old and was still full of fire. He returned to the college later to give his famous lecture, "The Book of Books," which he had delivered more than eight hundred times. And again he came to stay a month and lecture to the preacher boys on great preachers he had known: Spurgeon, Moody, and others.

Dr. Culpepper and Dr. Munhall would sit on the front row and yell, "Hear that," when a salient point was made by the preacher. We also heard our favorite preacher, our own "Dr. Bob."

It was not long after that Bible Conference that I felt the call to preach. At that time there were only six boys in the Student Ministerial Association. I made the seventh when I answered the call, and there were several others before the year was over.

I had a growing suspicion that God might want me to preach, but I refused to entertain the idea very long. But the preacher boys were going over to Millville in the college utility truck to hold a Sunday afternoon street meeting. They asked me to go along and give my testimony; so I went.

Millville had a harbor, and a lot of old salts sat round on benches, stools, and boxes along the street on Sunday afternoons. I gave a short testimony and closed it with an appeal for the men to be saved. At the close of the service an old fellow came and asked me to come with him around behind a little building to an alley. There he said, "Pray for me. I want to be saved." We knelt and prayed and he was saved.

That suspicion that God wanted me to be a preacher grew stronger, but I found it hard to surrender. The next day I was browsing in the college library and saw a book, *A Quest for Souls,* by George W. Truett. I checked it out, took it to my room, and read it. Dr. Truett told the story of a man on death row saying to a personal worker, "Man, if I believed as you believe—that if I die without faith in Jesus Christ I would be lost forever—I would be willing to crawl on my knees and tell people to repent and turn to Jesus Christ before it is too late." I do believe that; so an awful sense of responsibility came over me. I knelt by a dormitory chair and prayed but still was unwilling to be a preacher. I wanted to be a doctor.

The next morning at my first class after the roll call, the professor said, "I will ask Monroe Parker to lead in prayer." At my second class the same thing happened. I went to chapel, and the dean called me to the platform and asked me to lead in prayer. We were having spring football practice. That afternoon Coach Allison called us into a huddle and asked me to lead in prayer.

That evening I said to a fellow student, "Let's check out and go to town. I have got to get out of this atmosphere." We got up a load to ride the eight miles to Panama City in Leaping Lena, a T-model Ford which was run by L. C. Hendley as a jitney. We went to our favorite "chili joint" for a bowl of chili. I heard a man take God's name in vain; and before I hardly realized what I was doing, I found myself rebuking the man and trying to lead him to Christ. Something deep down in my soul told me that God wanted me to preach, but still I fought it. That night Marion Vickery said to me, "Let's get away and have some fun." I said, "All right, let's go to Birmingham." He said, "O. K. I will get permission to go home to Pensacola and will then come on to Birmingham."

The next morning I went to the office and told the dean I had to go to Birmingham because there was a terrific pain in my left side. When I got home, I told my people that I had come home for spring holidays. I had, but they were not official holidays.

"Vic" came to Birmingham via Pensacola, and I hitchhiked direct. We did have a lot of good clean fun but felt guilty for lying to the dean and leaving school; and when we got with a worldly crowd, we both felt sick.

One night my parents tried to talk with me about my college life, but conversation on that subject was difficult for me at that time.

Vic and I went to my room and tried to read. I think I read over the same page a dozen times. Finally we went to bed, but I could not sleep. I rolled and tossed, and at about two o'clock in the morning I woke Vic and said, "Let's go for a walk." We dressed and walked about a mile and a half from my house to a railroad. I said, "Vic, God is dealing with me about being a preacher." Vic said, "He is not calling me to preach, but he is dealing with me, too." We knelt down in the cinders for a long time. Finally I got up and looked up at the sky. It was a crisp February night, and the stars looked very near.

I held my right hand up toward Heaven and said, "God, Thy will be done." A wonderful peace came into my heart. Vic also made a commitment to God.

I could not sleep the first half of the night because I was so miserable; and when we got back to bed at nearly four o'clock, I could not sleep the rest of the night because I was so happy. It was not easy to wait until morning to tell my parents.

We started out hitchhiking for the college that very day. It took us three days to get there because of a flood. We were marooned in Troy, Alabama, a day and a night but finally made it back to college.

I walked into the dean's office and said, "Dean Patterson, I lied to you, sir. I told you that I had a pain in my side. The trouble was higher than I indicated. It was in my heart. God was calling me to preach. Please forgive me. I will take whatever penalty you give me and will make up my work if you will allow it." I thought I would be campused for the rest of the year. But the dean did not punish me. Of course, I had to make up the work I had missed.

CHAPTER X

Getting Started

A fter I talked to the dean, I went over to the dormitory and said to Henry Grube with whom I roomed for three years, "Henry, I am going to be a preacher." He said, "Good! you can preach next Tuesday night at Millville. The preacher boys are going to have a revival meeting there in the Methodist church. We will have seven nights, and we have only six preacher boys. You will make the seventh."

I said, "I don't know how to preach."

He said, "Just take a text and cut loose."

Well, I believe in preparation; so I made the best preparation I could. I found a text that gripped me—Philippians 4:13. I studied it in its context. Then I went to the library and read some commentaries on it. Then I made an original outline. If I should give it, you would know that it was original.

I went out in a Florida swamp near the campus to practice that sermon. I found a stump about the height of a low pulpit and got around so that the wind was favorable and the palmetto bushes would nod assent, and I cut loose. I preached to the bushes and the alligators and bullfrogs and the birds. Every once in a while an old bullfrog would say, "Amen."

I had that sermon down so that I could preach it in thirty minutes. Tuesday night before I went to the pulpit, a classmate, Clifford Lewis, put his arm around me and said, "Remember that Jesus said, 'Go preach the gospel and I will be with thee.'" I went to the pulpit, conscious of the presence of the Holy Spirit, and preached that sermon in seventeen minutes. I did not leave out a word I had preached to the bullfrogs. When I gave the invitation, ten people came forward to accept Jesus Christ as Saviour. That was March 7, 1929. Since then I have taken the hands of thousands who have come to be saved. The Sunday following the revival at Millville, I was invited to preach in Panama City; and the following Sunday, at the Presbyterian church in Lynn Haven; then the next Sunday, at the Methodist Episcopal Church in Lynn Haven.

Every Sunday until school was out, I had an invitation to preach in a different church. I preached on the same text—Philippians 4:13.

When school was out, Moody Holmes, who preached his first sermon in that revival at Millville where I preached my first sermon, and I went together to barnstorm the country. We were selling magazine subscriptions to make our way and earn money for our schooling the following year. That was the year the Great Depression came. The bankrupt business was no longer booming. My old job at the T.C.I. Commissary was open to me, but God had called me and I had committed myself to preach. My parents must have thought I had lost my mind when I wrote them what I was going to do.

Very few college students had cars in those days. We started hitchhiking from Dothan to Slocomb, Dr. Bob's hometown, a distance of twelve miles. We walked some distance preaching to each other as we walked down the wide, graded, clay road. Then we rode a couple of miles in a wagon, giving the Gospel to a dear old peanut and cotton farmer, and finally rode into Slocomb in a T-model Ford. We went to the Methodist parsonage to see if we could use the Methodist church building for a one-night service. The pastor was very inhospitable. He said, "Bob Jones does not even believe in evolution." We then went to the Baptist pastorium. The dear pastor, Rev. Mr. Gore, not only allowed us to use his church the following night but also invited us to stay at his home the two nights we were there.

We hurried to the printing shop and got a rush order of circulars to advertise the meeting. We went to the telephone office and got the operator, "Central," to call everybody in town and announce the service. We got some liquid chalk; and with permission from business people, we wrote the announcement on store windows and concrete walks. In this, Dr. Jones' hometown, our advertisement read:

HEAR
BOB JONES
COLLEGE PREACHER BOYS AT THE
SLOCOMB BAPTIST CHURCH
TONIGHT AT 7:30

We had a wonderful crowd. Moody led the singing and preached a short sermon to the young people, and I preached on "I can do all things through Christ which strengtheneth me" (Phil. 4:13). A goodly number were saved. We did not take offerings as I would if I had to do it over, but we announced that we would be coming from door to door the next day to take subscriptions to a Christian periodical.

We went next to Hartford, Alabama, where the Methodist pastor received us gladly; then to Crestview, Florida; Pensacola, Florida; Brewton, Alabama; Monroeville, Alabama; Thomasville, the place of my nativity; and Livingston, Alabama. Here we not only preached in the evening but also preached in the Livingston State Normal College for summer school chapel.

Then we went to my home for a few days where Pastor Baker received us with real enthusiasm. We had a good meeting here and preached on Sunday. Then Moody left me and went home to Dothan. I resumed the campaign with a foray into Mississippi. I went to Amory, Fulton, and Tupelo.

On a Wednesday afternoon, having sent in all of the subscription money, I was flat broke. I started out hitchhiking, thinking, "I will get to Aberdeen in time for prayer meeting. I will get there early so that I can make arrangements for a Thursday night meeting, and the pastor can announce it at prayer meeting. I will sell a few subscriptions after the service and will

have money to spend the night at a tourist home." A room in
a tourist home would cost fifty cents for a single person in those
days. But I got out on the highway wearing the only clean suit
of clothes I had, a summer suit of crash material. Then came
a hard summer shower. I got to Aberdeen wet, grimy, and
hungry, too late to go to prayer meeting. I was wearing
suspenders and a belt; so I sold my belt to a man on the street
for fifteen cents and bought some buns for supper. Then I went
to the little depot to spend the night. At 11:00 P.M. the town
marshal came to lock the door to the depot. I told him I wanted
to sleep in the depot. He told me to go to the hotel; and when
I told him I did not have any money, he called me a vagrant.
I argued with him about that. If he had said, "You are fragrant,"
I would not have argued; but he said, "You are a vagrant." He
won the argument. His verdict was, "You get out of town or go
to jail." I chose to get out of town. But since there was no traffic
at midnight, I walked down the railroad, leaving town thanking God that I was counted worthy to suffer for Him.

About a mile out of town, there was a pump house. The door
was open; so I went in, lay down on the rough floor, and pillowed
my head on my big, precious-promise Bible and went to sleep.
At five o'clock in the morning, a man came in to turn on the
steam. He punched me with his foot and woke me up. He was
dressed like Tom Mix, the movie cowboy. He had on a black out-
fit with high-heel boots and a ten-gallon hat and was wearing
a six shooter. I got up and opened my pillow to lead him to Jesus
Christ. He had been out all night playing poker and had been
drinking but was sober. He accepted the Lord Jesus Christ as
his Saviour. He knelt down on that old rough floor and poured
out his heart to God. With tears running down his cheeks, he
said he would go home and tell his Christian wife. He said she
would have breakfast ready for him. She would have bacon and
eggs, hot biscuits, butter and molasses, and black coffee. But
he forgot to invite me. Dirty, hungry and broke, I stood and
watched him go off down the railroad, and I was the happiest
man in the world. I knew why I had been kicked out of town.

I caught a ride to Birmingham and got home at about 2:00 P.M. Mother was out in the back yard hanging up clothes. A pot of butter beans left from lunch was still warm on the old wood stove. I sat down and ate every bean in the pot before I went out to kiss my mother.

After a few days at home, I hitchhiked back to Panama City, where Clifford Lewis had arranged for the preacher boys to preach for a week in July in a little chapel over the fire hall. Graff Parish had been appointed the pastor of the Methodist church at Millville. This was before he was married, and he had a parsonage but no furniture. Six of us were there. We slept on the floor. For breakfast we ate uncooked oatmeal with canned milk and drank coffee boiled in a syrup bucket. We were invited out for the other two meals each day, thank God.

One morning nobody was at the service but the six ministerial students and four godly women. Since it was Graff Parish's time to preach, he went ahead and preached the sermon he had prepared. It was on Hell.

CHAPTER XI

Revival Meetings

I went to General Delivery, and there was a letter from my mother telling me that our good pastor, Brother Baker, had arranged for me to hold a revival meeting at Newberg, Alabama. This was late in July, and the meeting was to begin Sunday night, August 4. I went home to make preparation. Among other things, I was licensed to preach by Dr. Branscomb, the presiding elder of the Bessemer District of the Methodist Episcopal Church, South, on Monday morning, July 29, one year to the day after I was saved.

The following Saturday Pastor Baker drove me up to Newberg. By this time I had three sermons. The meetings were to run through Friday night with services each morning at 11:00 o'clock and each night at 7:30. Brother Baker preached on Sunday morning, and I started Sunday night. I preached Sunday night on the text, "I can do all things through Christ which strengtheneth me" (Phil. 4:13). As I read the text I thought, "I can have a revival through Christ."

Monday morning I preached on the text, "One woe is past; and, behold, there come two woes more hereafter" (Rev. 9:12). I thought, "One sermon is past; and behold there come two sermons hereafter." That night I preached on the text, "It is finished" (John 19:30). It was finished as far as my repertory of sermons was concerned. I got up early Tuesday morning and prepared a sermon. It was not very well prepared. I am able to speak extemporaneously without difficulty and could do so then, but I like thorough preparation. Somebody said, "Open your mouth and God will fill it." He will—with wind.

But I had the best preparation I could in the time I had, and I expected God to bless although I did not see how He could do much with that sermon. But He blessed without the sermon.

When I got to the church, the dear old pastor, Brother Campbell, said, "We have time to go out to that cedar grove over there and pray. There is some shallow ground over there." He meant that in the cedar grove there were some big, flat rocks with sand on top of them. We knelt in the sand and prayed. Brother Campbell was a wonderful man. He had sharp, black eyes, long, black hair, and a handlebar mustache. He, by the way, is the man who some five years later led Dr. Tom Malone to Jesus Christ. He seemed to think that you had to pray loudly enough to be heard audibly all the way to Heaven, and he almost was. He was heard all right.

When I got up to preach, I opened my Bible at my text and then said, "Let's have a few testimonies this morning." I did not do this as a subterfuge. I just felt led to ask for some testimonies.

One man got up and gave what to me was a real funny testimony. He said, "I got right with God last night. I have been so far backslidden I have held my fourteen-year-old boy in my lap to keep the pastor from calling on me to lead in prayer. But we went home after the service last night and had family prayer." The pastor said, "I shall not hesitate henceforth to call on him even if he is holding his wife in his lap."

Another man got up and said that he got right the night before. Then a dear old man got up and in a trembling voice said, "My name is Wasson. I have been superintendent of the Sunday school here for forty-six years. I was saved when I was a little child. Jesus went with me through the Civil War. I pillowed my head every night on the ninety-first Psalm. I am now standing on Jordan's stormy bank looking over into the promised land. When you have your revival next year, I will be over Jordan."

Then he sat down and I said, "All right, we will have one more testimony, and then I will preach."

A funny-looking man got up, wearing a loud-colored suit about two sizes too small for him. He looked scared and in his hands was twisting an old-time cap with a long bill. He blurted out in a high-pitched voice, "This is the first time I ever made a testify in my life. But my little baby died last week and I want to be saved."

I said, "Come on." His wife said, "I want to be saved, too." I said, "You come, too." They knelt at an old-time mourners' bench as personal workers came to help them. I said, "Maybe someone else would like to be saved. Let's sing an invitation." Seven people came forward. When we finished leading them to Christ, it was too late to preach. I said to the old Confederate soldier-Sunday school superintendent, "Brother Wasson, would you come down here and stand with Pastor Campbell and me?" Then I said, "If you are going to meet Brother Wasson over Jordan, I want you to come and shake his hand. Then shake Pastor Campbell's hand and my hand if you wish."

They got in a pattern marching down to shake our hands. I did not know it, but another old Confederate soldier was there who would not speak to Brother Wasson, and Brother Wasson would not speak to him. They had got into an argument about something that happened in the War Between the States and had not spoken to each other for a long time. But this dear old man was also a Christian and would soon be "crossing over Jordan." He came down and was going to walk past Brother Wasson and shake hands with Pastor Campbell. But he had to look and see how Brother Wasson was responding; and for the first time in years, they looked each other in the eye. They stood there like two roosters about to fight, looking each other in the face. Then suddenly, seemingly simultaneously, they opened their arms and hugged each other and began to shout. Heaven came down and glory filled our souls.

The shouting was genuine. It was not the worked-up kind. That night people came in great numbers. The church was packed out. When I stood up to preach, I could see clusters of people outside each window listening. It was easy to preach. I felt like a preaching machine. The spirit of revival prevailed through the week, and many people were saved.

Invitations came for two more series of meetings, which I held before going back to college in September.

A well-known evangelist by the name of Collier was to hold a citywide tent meeting in Pratt City for two weeks in late August, and I was asked to preach to the young people each night at 7:00 o'clock. Then the regular song service would begin at 7:30. I had the privilege of preaching to the youth, but since everybody came at seven o'clock, we just had doubleheader services. The summer of 1929 was a great time for this fledgling evangelist.

Very often a young preacher will ask me, "How does one get started in evangelistic work?" I answer, "Son, there are two ways: you can start at the bottom and work up, or you can start at the top and work down."

CHAPTER XII

Return to College

I was eager to get back to Bob Jones College in September. Hitchhiking back to school through Clanton, Alabama, I saw a big black bullet-proof car pass and stop, and the driver signaled to the driver of a two-seated convertible in which there were three occupants. They picked me up, and I sat with the driver in the front seat. There was a third car in the entourage. It was like the lead car. One man in the car with me had a tommy gun, and one had an automatic pistol. They looked as if they were dressed for the race track, and they talked in the lingo of Chicago gangsters. They said they were from "Shy" and were "wit dem guys in dose cars." I will never know why they picked me up. I rode about 150 miles with them. They let me preach the Gospel to them nearly all the way. I asked them to let me out at a road fork about nine miles north of Cottondale, Florida, as they were headed for South Florida down the other road. They said, "No, we'll let you out in Marianna." Since Marianna was about the same distance from Cottondale as that fork, about nine miles, I sat tight.

About two miles from that point, the lead car stopped. They all stopped and all got out. The boss in his natty-looking dark suit and wide-brimmed hat said, "I want dem chickens." There was a flock of chickens near the road and about one hundred yards from a farmhouse. For a few moments it sounded like a young war. I have never seen so many feathers fly in my life—except when Henry Grube threw a pillow at Selwin Bradley one morning in our room and it burst open. They picked up the dead chickens, some of them still jumping, and put them in the trunk of the boss's car.

Once when the late converted gangster, Missionary George Mensik, and I were having chili together, I told him about that experience. He got excited and said, "I was dare! I was in dat back car! Dat was Capone's gang! We wintered in Florida. We cooked dose chickens at a tourist camp. We killed a calf after dey let you out. I remember all of dat." So I had preached the Gospel to three of Al Capone's gang.

Bob Jones College was located eight miles from Panama City and a mile from Lynn Haven, and we could catch rides on that route. But there was a shortcut from a point called Nehi about eight miles north of Panama City. From that point there was a seldom-traveled sandy road running a distance of two and a half miles to the college. When I left the gang at Marianna, I caught a ride to Cottondale and another one to Nehi. I could have ridden on to Panama City, but I preferred the shortcut. When I began walking down the sandy road, it was dark. I went all the way without having a single vehicle pass. When I was about a mile from the college, I could see the lights of the campus through a clearing. I was so eager to get there that I ran all that way carrying a large suitcase in each hand. Lest you think a young lady inspired this eagerness, I knew that my girl friend would not be returning to college. She dropped out to teach school at Milton, Florida. I went over to see her occasionally. Later we broke up.

A Busy Year

The academic year 1929-30 was a busy time for me. I was president of the student body, was active in the Chi Delta Theta Literary Society, which I served as sergeant-at-arms, and was fullback on the football team; I boxed and ran the cross-country racetrack and took a heavy academic schedule. The first year I was at Bob Jones, I was on the debating team of Chi Delta

Theta. But we lost the annual debate to William Jennings Bryan Literary Society. I was in several plays: *The Importance of Being Earnest, Suppressed Desires, The Patsy, Everyman,* and others. While I took speech every year, I dropped out of the plays so that I could go out and preach somewhere every week. The Bible Conference that year brought to our campus Dr. W. E. Biederwolf, a dynamic and scholarly evangelist; Dr. E. J. Pace, cartoonist and Bible teacher par excellence and creator of the Little Jets in the *Sunday School Times;* Mr. Worsham, a layman from Dallas with a great testimony; and W. I. Carroll, former assistant and successor to C. I. Scofield as pastor of the Scofield Memorial Church.

In the summer of 1930 I had a full schedule of revival meetings at Pinson, Palmer, Remlap, and Acipico and two in Pratt City. The meetings at Pinson were in the Mt. Pisgah Methodist Church. A comparatively young man by the name of Gibbs was the pastor. He was a dear brother in Christ and gave encouragement to a still younger preacher. At his invitation, I invaded his limited library and read several of his books. I suppose that since that summer I have done this with pastors a thousand times. Some of the libraries have been quite extensive. I have found in over fifty years of evangelistic work that one of the real sacrifices an evangelist must make is to be away from most of his books.

I walked every evening before the service in the old cemetery located next to the church and read epitaphs and prayed, a favorite activity of mine. I have done this in many graveyards. Our efforts in the meetings at Pinson were crowned with many souls and revival in the church. I was recommended to Brother Gibbs by Miss Bernice Rainey, a student at Bob Jones College. Brother Gibbs recommended me for meetings later in the summer to the churches at Palmer and Remlap, two communities about four miles apart. Remlap is Palmer spelled backwards. I was recommended by Brother R. L. Baker to Pastor Newton of the Acipico Methodist Church to lead a youth-sponsored revival meeting in his church. Talented young musicians were brought in, one of whom has since headed the music departments in two of Birmingham's schools of music. We had great crowds of people, both young and old, and saw many decisions for Christ. The same was true of all my meetings that summer.

CHAPTER XIII

Senior Year

T he academic year 1930-31 was another busy one for me. I was honored to be elected president of the Student Ministerial Association, which by this time had over forty men in it. I regarded this as my highest honor while in college although I had held other offices including president of the student body, alternate captain, and captain of the football team. Marion Vickery and I ran the snack shop, and he was the postmaster of the college post office, which was designated College Point, Florida. During football season I worked only after supper, when we opened for a few minutes, and from 9:30 to 10:00 P.M. The students were supposed to be in the dormitories studying from 7:00 to 9:30 P.M. Of course, there were exceptions for students practicing music, plays and programs, evening classes, studying in the library, working, and other responsibilities.

I held five series of meetings in small churches in the area during the academic year, and during the second semester I supplied the pulpit of the First Baptist Church of Panama City. In the spring of 1930 I had preached my first radio sermon on radio station WSFA in Montgomery, and several letters of commendation which I received encouraged me greatly. Below is a copy of one from Mr. J. A. Johnson of Georgiana, Alabama, dated January 4, 1931.

Georgiana, Ala.
Jan. 4, 1931
7:30 p.m.

Rev. "Monk" Parker

Dear Friend:

You will be surprised to get this letter. This is Ulay's father. I have heard Billy Sunday in Atlanta and Mobile about a dozen times. Have heard Dr. George Truett many times in conventions. Have heard Dr. Torrey several times. Have heard Dr. Bob many times. I have heard "Monk" Parker *one* time and that on radio. Dr. Truett has been complimented enough to spoil an average preacher, but he won't spoil. I stated in Sunday school today he was like John the Baptist, humble, not even worthy to unloose the shoes of Jesus.

I am about to say, in my judgment, your work is destined to be in a class with your teachers Dr. Bob and the above. I have told several times some of the things you said on "I can do all things. . . ." I wish you had time to write me in detail how you were converted and a synopsis of your sermonette on above text. Believe me—I appreciated that. I have two sons: Alvin, 24, graduate at Auburn in electrical engineering, was 16 months in Chicago, but out of work now and at home (he acted as superintendent in Sunday school today); and Ulay, a splendid boy. I told the Sunday school I would rather they could do what you could than be President of the United States. I am wondering if you would not like to hold a meeting here at Wesley Chapel. I judge you are a Methodist Episcopal. I am a Baptist; family, Methodist Episcopal.

This church holds its revival the second Sunday in August. I am enclosing $1.00, will buy you a little postage.

The good Lord bless you and make in you a great soul winner.

Your Friend,

J. A. Johnson

In the spring of 1931 Dr. Jones sent the graduating senior men, of whom there were only four, to Montgomery to broadcast, each for a two-week period. The Bob Jones College Prayer Hour was the first program on station WSFA each morning at 6:00, and the Bob Jones Revival Hour was daily at 3:00 P.M. Dr. Cassady, pastor of the Capital Heights Methodist Protestant Church, had charge of these programs for several years and was the regular preacher. He had many funny stories about each of the students who was sent up to broadcast. He loved to tell about the time Clifford Lewis was standing before the microphone preaching away, and the electric power went off. The operator signaled that he was off the air, and Clifford said, "Excuse us, friends. We are off the air and will be back in a few minutes." Once when a group of the old preacher boys were together, this was told on Clifford, and he denied it. One of the fellows said, "I know it did happen, too. I know because I was listening to the program that day."

A lot of people used to get "mike fright." This is like "stage fright" but occurs in the presence of a microphone. One old preacher who had never seen a microphone before came into the studio one day, and Dr. Cassady told him that he was going to call on him for prayer. He said, "Now, don't pray as loudly as you would from the pulpit. Just stand so that your mouth is about a foot from the microphone and pray at a conversational level." When Dr. Cassady called on him, he said, "Our Heavenly Father—is that about loud enough, Dr. Cassady?"

Once when I was preaching in the Montgomery area, Dr. Cassady attended the service and sat on the front row. A child back on about the fifth row was asleep and began to snore so loudly that it was disturbing the service. I said, "Will somebody wake up that child?" Dr. Cassady spoke up and said, "You wake him up yourself. You put him to sleep."

While my roommate Henry Grube was in Montgomery, Jimmie Johnson, who was an underclassman at the time, came and stayed in my room with me. He went with me when I went to preach on the weekends. One night while he was rooming with me, we discussed the call to preach, and I asked, "Jimmie, don't you think God is calling you to preach?" He fell on his knees by the side of our bunk bed and yielded his life to preach the Gospel.

Dr. Jones had left the preacher boys in charge of chapel for a two-week period. Since I was the president of the Student Ministerial Association and had charge of the program, I had Jimmie to give his testimony in chapel the next day. The whole student body was stirred. During those two weeks seven boys answered the call to preach.

Following the Bible Conference in February 1931, Dr. Jones sponsored Billy Sunday, who had preached in the conference, for a week of meetings in Alabama. He had sent advance men up to Alabama to visit the pastors for the cooperation of all the fundamental churches. Mr. Sunday preached in a large auditorium in Montgomery every night; and in Dothan, Selma, Birmingham, Troy, and Tuskegee in single daytime services.

Since my roommate Henry Grube and I were seniors, Dr. Jones allowed us to go with the party and help with some of the details for a few days. We rode in the car with Mrs. Stover and "Ma" Sunday. Billy Sunday and Governor Bibb Graves rode in Dr. Bob's car. Henry and I considered this one of the greatest privileges we ever had.

My second wife Marjorie, who was Dr. Jones' private secretary for seventeen years from the time she was a college sophomore, became a good friend of Mrs. Sunday, who survived her husband many years and served on the Bob Jones College Board of Trustees. In later years Mrs. Sunday usually came to our home for a visit when she came to Bob Jones University at Commencement time.

Great Preachers

With the exception of Dr. Jones, Billy Sunday was the most dynamic preacher I ever heard. With the exception of Dr. Jones, Paul Rader—the great radio preacher from Chicago, one-time pastor of Moody Church, and founder of the Chicago Gospel Tabernacle and Maranatha Bible Conference—was the most magnetic preacher I ever heard. With the exception of Dr. Jones, Dr. H. C. Morrison was the most dramatic preacher I ever heard. Dr. Jones combined the dynamic, the magnetic, and the dramatic in one personality; and with spiritual perception, a keen insight into the Word of God, and a homey philosophy, he outpreached anybody else I ever heard. But all of these men were great preachers; and in my opinion, when it comes to preaching, these men along with several others I have known stand out like California redwood trees over scrubby little bushes in comparison with many men who are called great preachers today.

A Tough Time

When the Great Depression came in 1929, it had a devastating effect upon the bankrupt business in which my father was engaged. A bankrupt sale was no longer sensational. Every business slashed prices and sold stuff cheap. But money was scarce. My parents were unable to pay my college expenses although from time to time they sent me a little money.

When I stepped on the campus in September 1930, I had seventeen cents in my pocket. All of the money I received for my meetings that summer I used to pay debts I had incurred the year before. I went to see Dr. Jones to ask for the special privilege of paying my bill at the end of each month instead of in advance.

One Saturday afternoon just after lunch, I sat on the edge of my bed, the lower level of a bunk bed, reading the Bible. I turned to the fourth chapter of Philippians and read the nineteenth verse, "But my God shall supply all your need according to his riches in glory by Christ Jesus." I pondered that verse and my plight. It was Saturday. I would have to have forty dollars by Monday or leave school.

As I sat there, I laid the Bible down on the bed by my side and crossed my foot on my knee. There was a hole worn almost through the sole of my left shoe. I began to fool with it and punched the hole through. I could not hold back the tears. There I sat, a big college man, weeping like a child. Then I picked up my Bible and looked again at that precious promise, and it shone like jewels through my tears, "But my God shall supply all your need according to his riches in glory by Christ Jesus" (Phil. 4:19). I said, "Forgive me, God. I don't have anything, but I am Thy child."

> My Father is rich in houses and lands,
> He holdeth the wealth of the world in His hands!
> Of rubies and diamonds, of silver and gold,
> His coffers are full, He has riches untold.
> I'm a child of the King, a child of the King:
> With Jesus my Saviour, I'm a child of the King.

I got up off that bunk bed, washed my face, shined my shoes and put some cardboard in the bottom of the one that was worn through, and went downtown to the bank to borrow money. As I walked into the bank at about two o'clock, the tellers' windows closed. I said, "It is not time for the bank to close." The bank was usually open until three o'clock on Saturday. An official said, "The bank is broke." I said, "So am I."

I started back to the college but decided to pay a friendly visit to Dr. Leckenby, who was pastor of the First Presbyterian Church in Panama City. Dr. Leckenby was a strong fundamentalist once associated with Dr. W. E. Biederwolf.

I did not tell him of my plight, but he invited me to preach for him the next day. When I was in college, a student did not expect an honorarium when he preached. It may be that some one or two people would leave a dollar bill in your hand when he shook hands with you. Or if it were in the country, some old farmer would say, "Come out to my car. I have something for you." He would give you a bucket of syrup, or a slab of bacon, or a tow sack of string beans, or a cake. Occasionally the pastor would say, "I will ask one of the ushers to stand in the vestibule and take a retiring offering for Brother Parker." One was not ever able to retire on a "retiring" offering. But on the day I preached for Dr. Leckenby, I received an honorarium which was more than enough to pay my bill at the college and get a pair of shoes.

There were only eight students in the graduating class of 1931, the first four-year graduating class. My seven classmates were:

1. Henry Grube, my roommate for three years. He was dynamic, unselfish, godly, enthusiastic, though at times morose, sharp, spiritual, original, and unique. He was greatly used of God. For forty years he signed his name Henry Grube, Romans 8:28. On the 8th month and the 28th day of 1968, he went Home to Heaven.

2. Rosetta Hardy, the daughter of a Methodist preacher, and a fine young lady who became a schoolteacher.

3. Mary Holcomb, a smart and friendly young lady. She also became a schoolteacher.

4. Fannie May Holmes, daughter of one of the finest couples I ever knew. She was a lovely young lady, modest though talented, and very appropriately became the wife of Bob Jones, Jr. She, of course, is known and loved by thousands.

5. Bob Jones, Jr., who went to summer school every year and got through high school in three years and also through college in three years. He was a little over two years younger than I, but we were the best of friends in college. The Joneses lived in a lovely home down on the bay front. Several times I spent the night with Bob. We were in some speech classes together, and one year we sat together in chapel. Before I went to Bob Jones College in the summer of 1928, Dr. Jones asked his congregation to pray for his son. I had just been saved. I began to pray for Bob then and have prayed for him daily ever since.

The high school boys took military training when the school was in Florida, and Bob had charge of this activity. He had been in Stark Military School his first years in high school.

Being the son of such an outstanding and dynamic man, who was the president of the college where he was a student, was not always easy for this young man. He had a great sense of humor and enjoyed carrying on a little mischief. I think that sometimes there was rebellion, not at being Dr. Bob's son, because he was always loyal to his father and justly proud of him and the things for which he stood, but against folks expecting perfection of him. He despised super piety and hypocrisy.

Then with his appreciation for the arts and being especially gifted in the area of drama, there was always the temptation to go in another direction.

Upon graduation, by the unanimous wishes of the College Board of Trustees, he became his father's assistant and taught speech and history and pursued graduate work in the University of Pittsburgh, from which he earned the Master's degree. In Cleveland, Tennessee, he became acting president. While Bob preaches with great fidelity to the principles of his father and with such power as characterized his father, he is properly credited with "putting the carpet on the 'Sawdust Trail.' "

As Acting President and later for twenty-four years as President of the University, he added to the curriculum cinema, opera and radio and created perhaps the greatest gallery of religious art in America. He brought into subjection to the Lord Jesus Christ all of these disciplines and has kept them there by training a staff and faculty with deep convictions and devotion to Christ.

6. Clifford Lewis, who began his preaching a few months before I began mine. He was a naturally born leader, an indefatigable worker, and one of the most consistent soul winners I ever knew. He was an inspiration to us all. We used to say that Clifford would shake hands with everybody in the world in his lifetime. If people had not kept being born after he passed their way, I think he might have made it. He preached his way around the world while he was in his twenties and has been everywhere. God took him to Heaven in November, 1985.

A fellow said to me, "Let's go around the world," and I said, "I am already here."

7. Ruth Mahan, who was active in the Life Volunteer Club. After graduation she went to seminary and then to Europe as a missionary. There she met and married the outstanding Scottish evangelist, the late James Stewart.

My first wife, Harriette. We married July 29, 1934.

"The Cutest Kid I Ever Saw"

Although I had dates with a good many girls during my senior year, since I was not "going steady," I sat alone during Bible Conference while this was a time of dating for most of the students. I got in the auditorium early to hear Billy Sunday and went down to the front row by the organ. Soon Harriette Stollenwerck, a seventeen-year-old girl, a cousin of Mrs. Bob Jones, Sr., who had been at Bob Jones College through high school and was now in college, came and sat down by me and said, "Hello, Monk Parker. May I sit by you? I am going to play the organ." I thought, *This is the cutest kid I ever saw.*

I went down to the front and sat with her for several more services.

About a month later a couple of us were going to Panama City one Sunday morning. Miss Katie Nell Holmes came to me at breakfast and said, "Are you going to Panama City? Harriette Stollenwerck has got to play the organ at the First Baptist Church, and I am going to chaperone her. Could we ride with you?" The car in which we were going was a coupe with a rumble seat. I let Miss Holmes ride up front, and I rode in the rumble seat with Harriette. I was making up a story so foolish I did not expect her to believe it about a lion hunt in Africa and had not finished when we arrived at the church; so I said, "We will finish this tonight in the dating parlor."

Although Harriette was only seventeen, she was a sophomore and was working on her sophomore recital in piano. One day Fred Brown and I were sitting next to each other in history class. It was a spring day, and the windows were open. The fragrant odor of prodigal flowers was wafted on the soft breezes, and in the distance I could hear Liszt's *Hungarian Rhapsody No. II* building to its exciting climax. I knew that it was one of her numbers. Then there was silence. I said, "Fred, I think I am in love with her."

He said, "Look out the window. There she goes."

I said, "I am going to find out."

I left the class without asking to be excused and called to her across the campus. She came over to me, and I said, "I wanted to see you. I have made a decision. I preach at Round Hill Saturday night and Sunday morning. I will be back Sunday afternoon and will come to see you Sunday night."

I prayed earnestly that God would have His way, but I felt that He had put it in my heart: this little girl would be my wife one day. When I told her on Sunday night that I loved her, to my surprise she answered, "I am glad. I love you back." The next day she wrote me a love note.

As soon, however, as letters had passed to home and back, she wrote me that she was too young to be in love, that we could be the best of friends. We assumed this relationship until her graduation in 1933, at which time we became engaged. We were married July 29, 1934.

CHAPTER XIV

After Graduation

T he day before I graduated in June 1931, Dr. Jones called me into his office and asked what my plans were. "Well," I said, "I am coming back for graduate work this fall. I have a meeting booked in July at the Methodist church in Excell, Alabama. I will get some other meetings and preach through the summer."

Dr. Jones said, "You have made a good record, and I am for you. How would you like to go to Anniston, Alabama, for the summer and go on the radio under the auspices of Bob Jones College? You could get a substitute while you are in Excell. A Mr. McWaters is opening a radio station in Anniston on June 10. It will be the first radio station in the city. He will let us have the first full hour each day from 7:00 to 8:00 a.m. for a sustaining fee."

He said, "We will do it this way. The first ten dollars to come in each week you can have to live on. All that comes in after that until the broadcast fee is met you send to the college to cover that fee which we will pay in advance. All above that you may have."

Anniston

I arrived in Anniston on June 8 with $5.00. I rented a room in a nice Christian home for $3.00 a week. I bought a $1.25 meal ticket at a restaurant. Hamburgers were five cents each in those days, and I lived mostly on hamburgers for a few days. I did purchase a loaf of bread and a can of potted meat. My beverage was mostly water.

I called on the pastors of the city and arranged for talent to help me with the broadcast. Since I had a one-hour period to fill, I divided that time into four periods. The first fifteen minutes I devoted to music and a message to Christians on prayer, soul winning, dedication, and related subjects. The second fifteen minutes I used for propaganda about Bob Jones College, my meetings, other meetings in good churches of the area, the broadcast, and other promotion. The third quarter of the hour we had musical numbers. Five churches furnished the music alternately. The fourth quarter of the hour I preached an evangelistic message.

When I called on Rev. O. A. Bonner, pastor of McCoy Memorial Methodist Church, he said, "We are starting a revival meeting in our church Sunday. A visiting pastor will do the preaching. How about your preaching to the young people each night in an early service?" I said, "I will be glad to." On the second night of the meeting the visiting pastor became sick and had to go home. I was asked to take over the campaign. During that meeting pastors attending the service invited me for meetings, and my summer was filled with revival meetings as well as broadcasting.

I got a Bob Jones preacher boy, Ed Hardin, to come take the radio while I was at Excell. Then I held meetings in the Methodist church in Glen Addie and in the Baptist church at Glen Addie and in the Oxana Methodist Church.

The last week that I was in Anniston I did not preach except on the radio. On the last Sunday night all the churches got together for a united service in the First Methodist Church, and I preached. Many came forward for salvation and many for dedication.

A Big Surprise

On Monday night of that week, I was invited to have supper

with some friends. After supper they said, "Let's go for a ride."
We got into their car, and they drove to the McCoy Memorial
Methodist Church. Cars were parked all around, and the church
was filled. They said, "Wonder what is going on in the church?
Let's go in and see." I did not suspect that this had anything
to do with me. The church was packed. People from all of the
churches where I had held meetings were there. The pastor
asked me to come to the platform. I thought I was going to be
called on to pray although the platform was filled with pastors.
In the choir loft were the various ensemble groups from the five
churches that had furnished music for me: First Baptist, Blue
Mountain Baptist, McCoy Memorial Methodist, Central
Presbyterian, and Oxana Methodist.

They had arranged a program in my honor. I was flab-
bergasted. Then the songleader announced a number. We stood
up and sang "There Shall Be Showers of Blessing." I sang louder
than anybody, too dumb to realize that they were giving me a
shower until the side door opened and in marched teenagers with
baskets of packages. I had so many pairs of underwear, shirts,
socks, and ties that I could have opened a haberdashery. When
I got back to graduate school, I had an auction sale in the dormitory and collected enough money to pay my brother James'
board and tuition for a couple of months. I got Dr. Stauffer,
pastor of the Central Presbyterian Church, to continue the Bob
Jones Hour. He did so for several years. He was a good fundamental, evangelistic pastor.

Since my parents were having a difficult time in the Depression, I took responsibility for James. He was a senior in high
school; so I took him to Bob Jones Academy.

CHAPTER XV

Graduate School to Evangelism

There were only three of us in graduate school: Henry Grube, Clifford Lewis, and I. However, we had a splendid faculty. We had homiletics under Dr. John Floyd Collins, under whom I had majored in English; Greek from A. H. Moore; and Hebrew and theology under Dr. Antonio Honorio Perpetuo, who had studied under Dr. Robert Dick Wilson at Princeton and had taught at Dallas, where he returned after teaching at Bob Jones.

Along in the fall, Dr. Jones called Clifford, Henry, and me into his office and said, "I was president of the International Association of Evangelists when we had over a thousand evangelists in that association. There is not much vocational evangelism today. I have contacts in every town in Alabama; and, of course, I have contact with a large number of evangelists. What would you think of my sponsoring an Alabama Statewide Revival Campaign in January and February?" We thought it was a great idea. He asked if we would be interested in holding some of those meetings. Of course, we would be.

Clifford Lewis had not actually enrolled in classes since he came to school late. He was auditing some classes and doing some independent study, waiting to start classes after Christmas. Since Henry had dropped Hebrew, Dr. Perpetuo doubled my time in Hebrew, making it possible for me to finish the semester by Christmas. Our other professors did the same.

Statewide Evangelism

Dr. Jones sent two advance men to Alabama to set up rallies in 120 towns. He went up to Alabama and held four rallies a day and challenged the churches to cooperate with the meetings he proposed. He had the advance men, Mr. Willis Haymaker and Mr. Roberts, to organize four series of thirty simultaneous campaigns, a total of 120 campaigns. Including Henry Grube, Clifford Lewis, Dr. Jones, and me, plus three college students—Jimmie Johnson, Red Hildreth, and Fred Brown—he brought thirty evangelists to Alabama, and each of us held four campaigns.

So it was that in January 1932 I left graduate school to go into full-time evangelistic work.

Dr. Jones had all of the evangelists to meet at the Whitcomb Hotel in Montgomery on Friday night before the campaigns began on Sunday morning.

My four campaigns were in Camden, Heflin, Marion, and Hamilton. The meetings in Camden were held in the courthouse. The local ministerial association had voted not to cooperate with the meeting. Rev. Mr. Kennedy, pastor of the Associate Reformed Presbyterian Church, was appointed to come see me and tell me so. He expected me to leave town.

I arrived in the little county seat town by Greyhound bus on Saturday afternoon and checked into the hotel. Mr. Kennedy came to my room to see me. After we introduced ourselves to each other, our conversation went like this:

Mr. K: "I have come to tell you that the four pastors of Camden voted unanimously not to cooperate with your meeting."

Myself: "I am very sorry to hear that. Why do you oppose the meeting?"

Mr. K: "There are three reasons. First, it is not an opportune time. January is too cold. Secondly, you will get students for Bob Jones College. Thirdly, you will take money out of town."

Myself: "First, Dr. Jones chose January and February for these campaigns because he did not want to conflict with your spring, summer, and fall programs. Second, I am not here to get students for Bob Jones College, but I would be pleased to get some of the right sort of young people to go there. Third, any moneys I receive will be given voluntarily without any pressure on the people. You would not object to a circus coming to town and taking thousands of dollars out of your town. If we have a revival, it will bring more money into your churches, and I expect to see a revival."

Mr. K: "Do you mean that you will go ahead without the cooperation of the pastors?"

Myself: "Of course. I came here to hold a two-week evangelistic campaign in the courthouse, and I would not think of leaving. Thousands of people are praying that God will send a mighty revival to Alabama. I expect to see it here in Camden."

Mr. K: "Well, I think you are making a mistake, but I say, God bless you."

Myself: "Do you mean that?"

Mr. K: "Why, yes."

Myself, kneeling by the bed: "Then pray for me now."

Mr. Kennedy knelt by my side and told God that he did not want to stand in the way of the Holy Spirit and asked God to pour out blessings upon the meeting. We got off our knees, and he with tears on his cheeks gripped my hand and said he would attend the meetings and help any way he could.

Mr. Kennedy went to see the other pastors. The Baptist pastor was out of town, but his wife agreed to attend the Sunday afternoon opening service. She was a wonderful pianist; and after that service, she volunteered her services and played the piano through the rest of the meeting. Her husband returned in the afternoon on Sunday, and she convinced him to call off the Sunday evening service. Nearly everybody in town attended the meetings.

Five High School Girls

The manager of the hotel where I was staying was Mrs.

Newberry. During the high school luncheon hour on Monday, Mrs. Newberry's daughter brought four other girls from the high school to question me about the dance.

"What is wrong with dancing?" the five of them wanted to know.

"Well," I said, "you have a doubt about it. Why don't you give God the benefit of the doubt?"

"Well, I don't see anything wrong with it," said Mae Newberry.

I asked, "Do you mean to tell me that you can be in a young man's arms, dancing to syncopated music, and not have any improper emotions?"

She said, "That's right."

I asked Edna Stewart. She said that she could.

Then I asked Elizabeth Duke, "What about you?"

She answered, "No, I will admit that I cannot."

Then Mae said, "I will stop for Elizabeth's sake."

All five girls knelt in the hotel parlor and gave their hearts and lives to God. They went back to school that afternoon and won many of their friends to Christ.

That afternoon I came out of the post office after getting my mail at General Delivery. I saw most of the high school students coming toward me. I thought they were headed for the post office; so I hurried across the wide sidewalk. The students turned and surrounded me and started asking questions about why Mae and her friends were stopping dancing. I took my New Testament out of my pocket and preached on the street. Four more girls were saved.

That night Jack Comack, captain of the football team in Camden that year, and Malcomb Stewart, Edna's brother, halfback on the football team, came to the service and said to me, "You are breaking up the dancing in Camden. All of the girls have said they will stop dancing."

I said, "Why don't you boys have a dance?"

He said, "That would not be any fun."

That night these two young men were saved. Malcomb later went to the mission field.

Many were saved in Camden.

Mae Newberry and her friends gave me a hand trunk which I used for years after that. Eighteen years after the Camden revival, I held meetings in the First Baptist Church in Thomasville, the church which was founded by Grandfather Parker. Those five girls, who were married and had Christian homes and were scattered over many miles, called me and said they were going to have a reunion and were coming together to my meeting in Thomasville and would like for me to have dinner with them at the Hill Hotel. We had a wonderful time, and it was a thrill to me to hear the testimony of each lady.

Heflin

The campaign in Heflin was held in the Heflin High School Auditorium. We had a good meeting although I had to get a substitute preacher for four nights as I had chicken pox during the second week.

Marion

The Marion campaign was held in the courthouse, which had ample room for a large crowd. The Baptist church was without a pastor, but the people responded wonderfully. I spoke in Judson College, a Baptist Women's College, and many students attended the meetings regularly.

The Methodist pastor, Rev. Mr. Pease, was an orthodox man and was regular in attendance, as were a large number of his people. Rev. Mr. Wallace, the Presbyterian pastor, was a strong fundamentalist and was evangelistic. His people were faithful.

I stayed in the home of Mrs. J. M. Smith, who was a great blessing to me. We had 165 professions of faith in this meeting.

Hamilton

The meetings at Hamilton were well attended until the Lindbergh baby was kidnapped. For several nights following that event, many people stayed at home as if glued to their radios. We reached a wonderful climax. I preached on the Second Coming. Most of the people had never heard of the personal, premillennial coming of Christ nor of the rapture of the saints. There was tremendous response to this.

From Hamilton I went home to Birmingham for a few days. Dr. Jones was in a meeting at Ensley which I attended a few nights. There were twenty campaigns (sponsored by Bob Jones) in progress in the Birmingham area, and all of the evangelists met with Dr. Jones for lunch each day at the Molton Hotel. We had a private dining room, and after lunch each man gave a report of his meetings.

Pittsburgh, Pennsylvania

From Birmingham Dr. Jones sent me to Pittsburgh, Pennsylvania, to broadcast on KQV, the second oldest radio station in America. There was an evangelist broadcasting for Bob Jones College who got that program in debt; so he resigned and moved to Washington, D.C. It was my task to try to get it out of debt and close the broadcast.

Dr. Jones said, "As soon as I get back to the college, I will send you a subsistence check and one each week. You send all moneys that come in for the broadcast to the college." He asked if I had enough money to get to Pittsburgh. I said that I did, but I had to send some money to my brother Jimmy, who was at Bob Jones College.

I rode a Greyhound bus from Birmingham to Pittsburgh, leaving Birmingham at midnight and arriving in Pittsburgh thirty-one hours later. I had only five dollars when I arrived. I walked from the bus station to the Y.M.C.A, where I was informed that

Pittsburgh. (1932) Broadcasting daily on the
second oldest station in America.

I could have a room for five dollars a week and would have to pay in advance. I asked if I could pay three dollars down and the balance later in the week. The clerk said that this was not allowed but that I could get a nice room for three dollars a week at the Allegheny Y.M.C.A. north of the Allegheny River. It was about three miles over there. I walked it in near zero weather, wearing a little thin topcoat. I had spent four winters in Florida, and my blood was thin; but with only two dollars above what I would need for room rent, I could not afford to ride a streetcar. I did not eat breakfast but spent thirty-five cents for lunch.

That afternoon I walked down to the building where the studio was located. It was on the top floor of a skyscraper in downtown Pittsburgh. The broadcast was at 3:00 P.M. We had a post office box, but I found it empty.

God Feeds His Sheep

Each day I would walk downtown and back for the broadcast and would stop at an armchair restaurant and get a hot roast beef sandwich with potatoes and gravy for thirty-five cents and sometimes a five-cent cup of coffee. But my two dollars ran out. Still I had received no mail. The check from the college had not come.

One very cold day when I had not eaten anything that day, I sat down at the microphone at three o'clock in the afternoon and preached on "The Lord is my shepherd; I shall not want" (Ps. 23:1). I went by the post office and found the box empty as usual. So I started back to the Y.M.C.A. over the Federal Street Bridge which spans the Allegheny River just above its confluence with the Monongahela, forming the Ohio. I stopped and put my hand on the steel rail on the banister and looked out over the frozen river. I did not see any green pastures. All I could see was white and black. It would snow a while and soot a while. When I started to take my hand away from the rail, the skin just above my glove had frozen to the steel. I pulled it away and said, "Lord, I thought You were my Shepherd. Well, if You are, I am a hungry sheep. If I had a hungry sheep and could feed him, I would do so."

I started on, and there in the snow was a little ragged purse from a lady's pocketbook. I picked it up, and it contained two buffalo nickels. I went back across the bridge to a White Castle hamburger stand and bought two hamburgers. They were five cents apiece in 1932.

When I got to the Y.M.C.A., the clerk at the desk said, "Fellow, you hit the jackpot." He poured out a large bundle of mail. My predecessor had had all of the mail forwarded from the post office box to himself in Washington, D. C. He wanted to be sure to get any mail intended for him personally. He had learned somehow where I was staying and sent the mail back to me. There were two weeks' checks from Dr. Jones and gifts for the broadcast from all over Western Pennsylvania, West Virginia, Ohio, and Western New York.

It was as if God leaned over the battlements of Heaven that day and said, "All right, son, if you can't wait until you get to the Y.M.C.A., here is a dime; go get some hamburgers."

I had rather have those two little buffalo nickels in my memory than to have a dividend check for a thousand dollars. That is in my memory.

CHAPTER XVI

Return to Alabama

I returned to Alabama in time for a Young People's Fellowship Club rally in Montgomery in April. Dr. Jones asked me how many Fellowship Clubs I could organize in two weeks in Southeast Alabama. I told him I thought I could organize one a day during the five school days of each week. He said, "All right, go organize them and arrange for a rally in the City Hall in Dothan two weeks from next Saturday morning, afternoon, and evening."

I went to Southeast Alabama and went to high schools and arranged to preach in chapel. I would announce that I wanted to meet at the noon hour or after school with the young people who would be interested in a club with a pledge to read the Bible every day, pray alone in secret two times a day, attend religious services whenever possible, especially prayer meetings, and to attend weekly meetings of the Fellowship Club set not to conflict with their local church programs. We organized fifteen clubs ranging from seven members at Kinsey to 112 members at Enterprise.

Dothan

Dr. Jones came for the rally and brought a group of students with him. We had a great day. Following that I held a week of meetings in the City Auditorium at Dothan.

York

In June I held a two-week meeting in the Methodist church at York, Alabama. The Baptists cooperated and made it a communitywide meeting. We had two services a day, and all places of business closed for the morning services.

My brother Jim had just graduated from Bob Jones Academy and would be returning to Bob Jones College in the fall. He came by to see me.

I had a rash on my chest caused by eating too many strawberries. I scratched it and got it infected. Thinking it was eczema, I put eczema remedy on it, and that irritated it. I would preach very hard in every service and would sweat so much that my clothes would stick to my sore chest; and the only relief I could get was to strip my chest and lie on my back and fan. Jimmy stood at my bedside and cried when he saw how I was suffering. I closed the York meetings on Friday night and went to Thomasville, Georgia, for a citywide campaign beginning on my twenty-third birthday, June 23, 1932.

The railroad from York to Montgomery had cut off passenger service, but they sold me a ticket and allowed me to ride in the caboose of a freight train. In Montgomery I caught a bus for Dothan, where I spent Saturday night. Jimmie Johnson and Fred Brown were in meetings not far away. Fred was to preach on Saturday night; so Jimmie came to Dothan for a visit with me. We had supper, and he left at about eight o'clock Saturday night. I was suffering from the infection covering the front of my body, by this time from my shoulders to my knees. I fell on my knees and cried out in pain, and said, "Lord, if You want me to go to Thomasville, Georgia, You will have to heal me. Otherwise, I will go to the hospital." Then I stood up and fell backwards on the bed with my clothes on, thinking I would get up in a few minutes and prepare for bed. But I fell into a deep sleep and did not awaken until eight o'clock Sunday morning. The infection and the pain were all gone. It was a miracle God performed in answer to prayer and to get me to Thomasville, Georgia, where He was to use me signally. I believe in Divine healing, but I do not believe in human "divine healers." All healing is divine, whether it is through sleep or rest or medicine or surgery or diet or physiotherapy or a miracle of God.

Thomasville, Georgia

When my train pulled into the station at Thomasville at 2:00 P.M. Sunday, all of the pastors and a great crowd of people were there to meet me. The opening service was at 3:00; so I had just enough time to get settled in my room and make it to the service. The campaign ran for three weeks. The plan was for the meetings to be held the first week in the First Baptist Church, the second week in the First Methodist Church, and the third week in the First Presbyterian Church, with all three churches attending each week; but the crowds were so large that we returned to the First Baptist Church the third week.

A large vacant store building was equipped for daytime services, and most of the stores closed during that service each morning.

I gave the first invitation on Tuesday night of the first week and 111 people came forward for salvation. According to Mr. Smith, chairman of the personal work committee, that was the smallest number to respond to the invitation during that 22-day campaign. The songleader was Mr. W. G. Stracenor. During the meeting he came forward to answer the call to preach. He gave up his job as director of the Y.M.C.A. and went out to Pavo and pastored a little church for fifty dollars a month. From there he was called to the Baptist church at Madison, Florida, and then to Riverside Baptist Church in Miami, which was the largest church in Florida. For many years he has served as editor of the *Florida Baptist Witness*.

In the Thomasville campaign, Raymond McKendry was converted. He was a ministerial student in a modernistic school. He was a junior and had been elected to edit the yearbook in that college the following year. He came to me and asked, "Where did you get all of your crazy ideas?" I invited him to my room and led him to Christ. He transferred to Bob Jones College that fall.

A Greek boy whose father was a peanut vender on the street corner was saved and went to Norman Park College to study for the ministry.

Eva Pedigrew was saved and went to Moody Bible Institute to study for the mission field.

Estell Johnson, who later married a Mr. Joiner, a dairyman in Jacksonville, Florida, was saved. She has attended my services in recent years as I have preached in several different Jacksonville churches. She has served for many years as organist and as superintendent of the intermediate department of the Sunday school in the large Broadway Baptist Church in Jacksonville.

In the Thomasville meetings Dorothy Davis was saved. She went to Bob Jones College and majored in organ. She married my brother Jimmy and gave him five lovely children, two daughters and three sons. All three sons are in the ministry, two of them preaching and the other in the ministry of music. Dorothy's father, Mr. J. B. Davis, was converted. This was in the depth of the Depression. Mr. Davis operated the All-American Cafe. He promised God that if He would help him get Dorothy through Bob Jones College, he would help other worthy students if in need and if he could. He kept that promise and helped students until his Homegoing a few years ago. He used to write and ask me to recommend some worthy, needy student. He helped several at Bob Jones College and several at Pillsbury Baptist College who are in full-time Christian work.

These are just a few of many who were saved in our Thomasville campaign.

Boyleston, Alabama

From Thomasville I went to Boyleston, Alabama, a large mill

town in the Montgomery area. There we had a wonderful revival. Conviction fell all over town, even among people who had not attended the meetings, because of the prayers and the testimonies of those who had. I went into a drugstore one evening, and the druggist said, "You are the evangelist, aren't you? I have been hearing about the meetings. I have not been out myself. You see, I am a pharmacist and do not get to go to church. I suppose I could go. I go to ball games, and I go hunting and fishing. I guess a fellow finds a way to do what he really wants to do. I have just not wanted to go to church because I am not a Christian. Pray for me that I will be. I want to be saved."

I had not said a word to the man; but I stood there and listened to him lead himself to conviction, and then I led him to Christ.

In Boyleston a young man by the name of Deloach was converted. He invited me to come to the boardinghouse where he was boarding to have lunch. There were six men at the table besides me. Mr. Deloach said, "Fellows, we all know that we are sinners, but I was saved last night. At the table we have all dived into the food and eaten like hogs. We are going to stop that. We are going to pray before we eat." One man pulled back his chair and knelt by it. All of the others followed his example. All five of Deloach's friends got saved there at the boardinghouse table.

Years later Mr. Deloach's son James attended Bob Jones College and was in my preachers' class. Then twenty-three years after the Boyleston revival, when I was pastor at Grace Baptist Church in Decatur, Alabama, Mr. Deloach's sister, who was also saved in the Boyleston meeting, joined my church. The church in Boyleston had only 96 members, and we took in 112 members by profession of faith.

Following the Boyleston meeting, I went to Castleberry, Alabama, for a short meeting and on to Bob Jones College for the first annual Fellowship Club meeting in August of 1932. Dr. Jones, Clifford Lewis, Henry Grube, and I were the speakers. We had a wonderful conference with many young people attending from all over the southeastern states and several from other places.

Butler, Alabama

My next campaign was in the Methodist church at Butler, Alabama. I stayed in the home of my Aunt Marcita Dansby. Several of my relatives gave their hearts to Christ in that meeting, and there were many conversions. In fact, so many young people were saved that a local dance hall located near Butler had to close up. The following letter I received from my Aunt Marcita:

Dear Monroe:

I feel that I must write and tell you of some of the visible evidences of the good works you did while in Butler.

There was a splendid crowd at the Fellowship Club last Saturday night and from all reports they are really in earnest and mean to live up to the pledges. So many of them are boys and girls that have been dancing and playing cards, too.

Gene Lenoir came to me Sunday morning at S.S. and asked me to announce at the Baptist Church that she wanted to keep the "Booster Band" going that you started while in Butler and she would meet with them every Sunday afternoon. Then I cannot begin to tell you of the numbers of people who have been to me and said so many nice things about you.

You did more good than any preacher that has ever been here since I have been here. I am sure of that. I wish we all could have the opportunity of hearing you more often.

Several here heard you over the radio in Montgomery Sunday morning. The next time you broadcast be sure to let me know.

Monroe, I know you must get a great joy and satisfaction out of life. To me it is the most beautiful sight in the world to see a new consecrated young person. I never see one that I don't wish that I had lived a Christian life when I was young and had grown in the grace of the Lord; as it is I am nearly forty years old and still a "babe in Christ," you might say.

I am so glad you are praying for me. I am reading my Bible and praying every day myself and you know that is something I have never done before and yet I have always wanted to be a Christian.

We carried Josephine to Judson Tuesday a.m., stayed there about two hours, stopped by to see Leslie a while on our way back.

Josephine writes that she is happy and having such a good time at Judson. I feel sure that she will study and make good. Cliff's school starts Monday and I'll be so glad to have him in school again.

Had a letter from Mamie Jo today and she said she would be over Sunday.

Monroe, I want you to know it certainly was a pleasure for us to have you with us and I do sincerely hope we can have you with us again sometime. I know you have a wonderful future ahead. We are so proud of you. You must take care of yourself.

With love and best wishes,
Aunt "Cita"

Below is a copy of an editorial that appeared in the Butler County newspaper.

WHAT MANNER OF MAN IS THIS?

For the past week there has been among us in Butler a man whom it has been well for us to stop and ask ourselves, "What manner of man is this?" He has been going about and doing good and offering his services to all who might avail themselves of it, in an effort to free themselves of the bondage of sin.

This man is still in his boyhood, so to speak. He has just turned twenty-three years and life looks out broad ahead of him. True, he has accomplished much already, but picture his future. How long it will last, no one can say. But we do know this, that if he continues at the same rate that he has during the week he has been among us, he will accomplish more for the good of humanity in a short period than most men who live to ripe old age.

Four years ago the great God of this universe implanted into the heart of Monroe Parker, then a young man in college, the desire to preach His word. So carefully was that seed of desire nurtured that it consumed the entire make-up of this young man. Three years ago he started upon his ministry and today there are few men with much more experience ahead of them who are having more success in turning people away from the wrath to come.

Butler is glad that Rev. Monroe Parker has come its way. Every person who has heard him appreciates his worth to this community, but those who will thank him most are those who have been enabled through his ministry to start life anew.

Homerville, Georgia

Two men by the name of Clark and Bell had held meetings in Homerville, Georgia, and had organized a Christian Business Men's Club, patterned after the Billy Sunday Clubs. It should not be confused with the present-day charismatic Businessmen's Clubs. The leader of this group was Mr. Folks Huxford, who was editor of the local newspaper. There were five men who were opposed to our campaign, but Providence had moved them all out of the way before our meetings began. Three of them were dead; one had been taken to prison for an offense committed in another state some five years previously; and the other had been moved to another city by his employers. But the opposition to the meetings did not cease.

Prominent church members were involved in a terrible scandal. The wife and son and daughter of the man involved took the other woman, a church pianist, to another city, knocked her unconscious, and poured carbolic acid on her body. This happened during the campaign; and, of course, people were hard to reach. But there was deep conviction.

One night I asked all who would to go to the basement and pray that revival would shake the city. Only twenty-seven people responded, but they prayed earnestly and fervently. One young lady prayed that God would send revival even if He had to take unsaved loved ones to bring large numbers of unsaved people to Christ. I shuddered because I did not know whether she ought to pray like that. I still do not know, but I did know that God was tuned in to that prayer. The next afternoon that girl's unsaved half-brother died. I had talked to him that morning and pleaded with him to be saved. He said, "I will do it tonight."

I said, "You cannot decide this morning that you will be saved tonight. You cannot be saved tonight without repentance. Repentance is a change of attitude; and if you are willing to change your attitude tonight, you will do it right now."

He said, "I will do it tonight."

He died that afternoon in an awful convulsion while damning the name of God, and it seemed to affect the whole town.

When I got to the service that night, the building was packed. I could not get through the crowd on the outside; so I went to the back of the auditorium and climbed through a window. I was going to preach on "Sin, when it is finished, bringeth forth death" (James 1:15). But when I stood up to preach, I preached on John 3:16. When I gave the invitation, scores and scores of people came forward, and we saw revival in Homerville.

CHAPTER XVII

Bob Jones Gospel Centers

Dr. Jones decided to open a number of Gospel Centers over the country. He wanted some preaching centers for Bob Jones graduates. He sent me to Mobile to open one and Clifford Lewis to Pensacola. Mr. Don Cochran, who had been an advance man for Dr. Jones in many of his citywide campaigns, went to Mobile and procured the old bus station on Bienville Square on St. Francis Street across the street from the park in the heart of the city. He made it into a very nice tabernacle. He put up signs advertising the Bob Jones Gospel Center. We had good newspaper stories. The papers were friendly, and we were able to get little squibs in the daily paper announcing my subjects and reporting the results of the services. The Mobile *Register* even printed one of my sermons, beginning on the front page.

We opened the first Sunday in December and had services morning and evening every day in the week. The Depression was on, and scores of men were in the benches in Bienville Square. We went over and invited them to the services, and most of them came. However, for the first three weeks, our crowds were very small and the offerings were also very small. But I cannot recall a service in which somebody was not saved.

Christmas 1932 was the first Christmas I ever spent away from home. But looking back over my first year in full-time evangelistic work, I was very happy for this year during which many hundreds of souls had come to the Lord Jesus Christ.

January 1, 1933, I went on the radio in Mobile. This brought larger crowds to the Gospel Center. We filled the building, and by February we were having overflow crowds.

Pensacola

Henry Grube was holding forth in the Gospel Center that Clifford Lewis had started in Pensacola. Counting the radio, I was preaching three times a day. Henry was also on the radio in Pensacola. We agreed to swap places for a couple of months on March 1. So Henry went to Mobile, his hometown, and I went to Pensacola.

These centers were not rescue missions. They were more like revival campaigns. Several pastors in each city cooperated with us. We did not have Sunday morning services but preached in various churches on Sunday mornings. We had what we called mass meetings on Sunday afternoons, and we did have Sunday night meetings. Hundreds of souls were saved in the Gospel Centers, and we directed these converts into the good churches. Our problem was in getting evangelists to man the Gospel Centers. I returned to Mobile for the month of May, and Henry Grube went back to Pensacola for the month.

At the end of May, Fred Brown and Ed Hardin graduated from Bob Jones College. Fred went to Mobile for three months, and Ed went to Pensacola. Later Ed went into the Methodist pastorate, and Fred Brown has continued in full-time evangelistic work through these many years. At the end of May, I went down to Bob Jones College for Commencement. At the Bob Jones Board Meeting in 1933, I was elected to the Board of Trustees of Bob Jones College.

At that Commencement Harriette Stollenwerck graduated from college, and she and I became engaged. She was to teach piano and organ at the college the next year, and we planned to be married in the summer of 1934.

The college moved that summer from Bay County, Florida, to Cleveland, Tennessee.

"Monk" Parker, Evangelist. (1933)

Atlanta

My next campaign was in Atlanta, Georgia. It was sponsored by the Southern Evangelistic Association and the Atlanta Bible Institute. These two organizations joined in an effort to reach Atlanta for Christ. They engaged two large tents. Dr. P. W. Philpot, who had been pastor of Moody Memorial Church in Chicago and later the Church of the Open Door in Los Angeles and had founded a great church in Hamilton, Ontario, preached in the tent located on Peachtree Street. The tent where I preached turned out to be in a better location at Moreland and Glenwood Avenues. We ran three weeks, and the original plan was for me to have Saturday nights as rest nights, and Dr. Philpot was not to have Monday night services. However, since the crowds at our tent were so much larger than at the other tent, the committee asked me to take my people to Dr. Philpot's tent on both Monday and Saturday nights. I might say, though, that crowds were good in both places.

Radio was comparatively new in 1933, and we were scheduled on WSB, the *Atlanta Journal* Station that "covers Dixie like the dew." Dr. Philpot did not like to preach on the radio, but he loved noonday meetings. The committee had engaged the Capitol Theater for noonday services. We were to alternate in the preaching on the radio and at the theater. Dr. Philpot told me that if I would let him have all of the theater services he would appreciate it if I would take all of the radio services. I was glad to swap. This is what brought such good crowds to our tent although on the radio I pushed Dr. Philpot's services at the theater and at the tent on Peachtree Street.

God poured out rich blessings on all of the services, and many souls were saved. Thirty-five years after those meetings, I received a letter from a dear man and his wife who were converted in that campaign, thanking me for getting them to Christ. They were members of Pastor Raymond Seay's church, and Raymond told me of their faithfulness to Christ.

CHAPTER XVIII

Evangelistic Campaigns Continued

F ollowing the Atlanta meetings that summer, I held meetings at Jackson, Tennessee; Pinehill, Alabama; Orion, Alabama; Waycross, Georgia; Montgomery, Alabama; and Repton, Alabama. Also, I returned to Butler, Alabama, where I had held a meeting in the Methodist church and where Mr. Grube, Henry's father, had set up a countywide meeting for Henry and me.

Mr. Grube was a licensed Methodist preacher but was a traveling salesman. He was a good man. He traveled in Southwest Alabama. He got the pastors together, and they planned a countywide campaign to be held in the Baptist church with another service somewhere else throughout the county each night.

We also had morning services. Henry and I alternated in the preaching at the Baptist church. The one who was not preaching there preached in the auxiliary service. We also alternated in the morning service; and one morning we had my brother Jimmy, who was seventeen years old, to preach his first sermon. The campaign ran two weeks and was greatly blessed of God.

Simultaneous Campaign

The first year Bob Jones College was in Cleveland, Tennessee, Dr. Jones set up a countywide campaign for Bradley County with alumni and ministerial students preaching.

I conducted the campaign at the First Baptist Church in

Cleveland. Clifford Lewis was in the First Methodist Church. Henry Grube was in the Broad Street Methodist Church. James Zellner was in First Presbyterian Church; Fred Brown was at Ooltewah, Tennessee; Jimmie Johnson was at Benton, Tennessee; and various preacher boys were in country churches throughout the county.

Revival at Harrison, Tennessee

In December I held a meeting in Harrison, Tennessee, located in the valley which is now the bottom of Lake Chickamauga. Service after service I could sense satanic power at work but did not know what was the matter. I prayed much, and God answered.

I had noticed that people would raise their hands, and a lady who sat on the back row would go to them but never got any of them to come forward. One night pungent conviction fell on that woman. She came down the aisle with the old-fashioned shakes and fell on her knees. She went into convulsions and then got calm and stood up and said, "I have been doing personal work for the Devil. When people would raise their hands, I would go to them and persuade them not to come forward. I did not want our gang to give up their worldly practices." On the next stanza of the invitational song, all the people that young woman had held back came forward.

1934—Spartanburg, South Carolina

Dr. Jones said to me, "Monk, how about going to Spartanburg to start a Bob Jones Gospel Center. A businessman who dropped into the center in Mobile was impressed with it and has written that Spartanburg, South Carolina is wide open for such a ministry. The man who wrote is Mr. Bridges. I will give you his address."

I arrived in Spartanburg early in the morning New Year's Day, 1934, and checked into the Franklin Hotel. After a morning nap, for I had ridden a Greyhound bus all night from Birmingham, Alabama, on which there was a drunk man singing without ceasing, "Get Along Little Dogie, Get Along," I went out to look over the city.

I walked two or three blocks and saw a big sign announcing that Evangelist Norman Greenway would open a campaign in a large tabernacle the next day. I found the tabernacle, an improvised one in a large vacant garage building. There were benches for a thousand people. The floors were covered with wood shavings, and there were attractive gospel signs on the walls. I asked the caretaker how long Mr. Greenway planned his campaign. He said, "Eight weeks." *Well,* thought I, *this is a free-lance ministry here, but I will look up Mr. Bridges.*

Mr. Bridges was a patent medicine salesman. He was blind and had a big Indian man who drove him around to the mill villages where he peddled his medicine from door to door. But he was a member of the Billy Sunday Christian Business Men's Club. He took me to meet Dr. Crane and Dr. Brannan, dentists who had offices together. They invited me to speak to the Billy Sunday Club on Thursday night.

I Stayed

Well, I had gone to Spartanburg to start a Bob Jones Gospel Center; so I made up my mind that I would stay and see it through. But I could not pay for my room in the hotel and eat, too. I moved to the Y.M.C.A. and ate very little. At night I attended the Greenway meetings and met people who would attend the Gospel Center.

By Thursday my money had just about run out. I bought several oranges and ate them for lunch and saved the peelings for supper.

Thursday night I spoke to the Billy Sunday Club and explained the Gospel Center. About twenty-five men were there. They assured me of their cooperation. One man shook hands with me and left a nice bill in my hand.

I decided to hold meetings in communities in Spartanburg County until the Greenway meetings were over.

There was a community about seven miles from Spartanburg by the name of Disputana. Mr. Bridges let me drive his car and went with me to see a Christian man he knew who was the chairman of the Disputana school board. He allowed me to use the high school auditorium free of rent for revival meetings. I went door to door to every home in Disputana and invited the people out for evangelistic meetings to start Sunday afternoon.

At the Thursday night meeting of the Billy Sunday Club, I had met Mr. W. L. Hendrickson. He invited me to lunch on Friday at his home. He had four lovely daughters, three of whom later attended Bob Jones College.

I certainly enjoyed the steak dinner Mrs. Hendrickson prepared for us that day. I called the Hendricksons and asked them to come out to the meetings in Disputana. They and other Spartanburg people attended.

After the Disputana meetings, I was invited to hold meetings in Clifton, South Carolina.

The Greenway meetings continued eight weeks. Mr. Greenway was from Toronto, Canada, and was a splendid prophecy preacher. He had traveling with him a singer and a terrific pianist, Al Bane. He had to let his singer go, and he asked me to lead singing for him for the last two weeks. I am not a singer, but I could function as platform man, could heist a tune, and knew how to beat the measures. Then Al Bane's playing gave buoyancy to the services. There were about a thousand people in attendance each night; so I got acquainted with many fundamental, evangelistic people.

Greenway was a great violinist. He had contracted with broadcasting station WSPA to put on a thirty-minute classical violin program each afternoon at three; and as compensation, they would give him thirty minutes each morning for a gospel program. When his campaign was over, he took me down to meet the station manager and asked him to let me take the morning time although he would not be putting on the afternoon program.

The station manager was leaving for New York, but he called in the program manager and said, "This is Evangelist Monroe Parker. Put him on next week from 8:00 to 8:30 in Mr. Greenway's place."

After three weeks he returned from New York and heard me on the radio. He called his program manager and asked, "Who is that?" He said, "The evangelist you told me to put on in Greenway's place." He said, "I meant for you to put him on for one week." The program manager said, "Well, he gets more mail than all the rest of the programs put together."

The station manager asked me to come into his office when my broadcast was over. He said, "We are going to have to charge you for your time from now on." The rate would have been several hundred dollars a month, and I said, "I can't pay it. Could you leave me on for a sustaining rate of thirty dollars a week?" After a long period of meditation, he agreed to do it.

Gospel Center in Spartanburg

I had bought Mr. Greenway's benches, ninety of them fourteen feet long. Since Greenway's building was no longer available, about two blocks from where Greenway had held his meetings, I rented a vacant garage building that would seat a thousand people. Many friends helped me get it ready, painting the walls white, building a large platform, moving the benches, cleaning the floors, equipping the office, and other necessary jobs.

We opened Thursday night, March 1, 1934. While I had marked time for the Greenway meetings, I had started seven Young People's Fellowship Clubs in Spartanburg County. All of the clubs came in delegations for the opening night. In the clubs from Disputana and Clifton, there were a large number of young people whom I had led to Christ. Many of them gave testimonies. The Disputana Club surprised me with the gift of a beautiful wristwatch which they presented in that service. We had good crowds for the first few weeks, but some people tired of coming every night week after week. I invited Dr. Bob Jones to come over and preach for a weekend in the spring. I was determined to have an overflow crowd for him; so I arranged for many delegations and advertised widely but cheaply. I got some cards a foot long and six inches wide with only three words printed on them, "Hear Bob Jones." I got permission to tie them on telephone and telegraph poles and tied one on each side of every pole in downtown Spartanburg.

Everywhere one would look he would see, "Hear Bob Jones." Newspaper stories identified Bob Jones. The building was packed, and many stood outside. We had wonderful crowds in the spring, and many were saved.

Meetings in Bowling Green, Kentucky

I went to Bowling Green, Kentucky, to hold a revival meeting in April and had a wonderful time. Dr. E. C. Comfort, the pastor, was a good man. He arranged for me to preach in Western Kentucky State University and in the Bowling Green Business College. I preached to 2500 people at Western Kentucky on the blood of Christ. A missionary's son from China by the name of Addison Talbert was saved and transferred to Bob Jones College and went into the ministry.

Eric Folsom supplied the Gospel Center for me for several weeks. I went down to Dixon Mills, Alabama, and held a meeting for Eric's father in June. In July a Bible Conference was held at the close of summer school at Bob Jones College. Clifford Lewis, Henry Grube, and I were speakers, along with Dr. A. T. Robertson from Louisville, Dr. H. C. Morrison, Dr. Bob Jones, and Mrs. Tom Torwater.

The last evening of the conference, July 29, six years to the day after my conversion and five years to the day after I was licensed to preach, Harriette Grace Stollenwerck and I were married. Cullen Biddle, who lived in Knoxville, drove us there that evening, where we stayed at the Farragut Hotel. From there we went to Spartanburg, where we rented an apartment.

Chapel at My Alma Mater

In October I was engaged to preach in chapel at Bob Jones College for two weeks while Dr. Jones was in meetings in Ireland. I left the Gospel Center in the hands of Rev. George Reeves, pastor of the Northside Baptist Church. The Depression was on, and several large cotton mills closed down. The offerings fell off. I was scheduled for other meetings. Mr. Reeves was discouraged and closed the Gospel Center. Later an evangelist by the name of Leaman went to Spartanburg; and with the help of a fine layman, Mr. Allen Rogers, led most of the Gospel Center crowd in establishing a tabernacle church. Mr. Leaman was overextended financially and left, but the church continued.

My ministry in the Spartanburg Gospel Center was like one long evangelistic campaign, beginning March 1, 1934, and running through September. During this time I was out of that pulpit five weeks while away in meetings. I preached 206 sermons in the Gospel Center, 25 sermons in various churches throughout the area, and 125 radio sermons, a total of 356 sermons in those seven months, and was away five weeks in evangelistic meetings.

Following the ministry at Bob Jones College, in October I went down to Pensacola to participate in the second anniversary of the Gospel Center. Clifford Lewis, Henry Grube, Fred Brown, Eric Folsom, Ed Hardin, Hiram Paul Mathison, and I were all there in a kind of reunion. Clifford, Fred, and Eric had not married at that time. Harriette, Eldora Grube, Katherine Hardin, and Bobby Mathison were there and furnished wonderful special music.

After the anniversary in Pensacola, Henry, Ed, and I and our wives went to Mobile for the second anniversary there. Then Harriette and I went up to Thomasville, Alabama, the place of my nativity, for a week's meeting in the Methodist church.

Returning to Mobile in late November to preach a few nights at the Gospel Center, I was convinced that I could no longer remain in the Methodist Church.

I believed the Baptist distinctives:

The Bible is the only authoritative rule of faith and practice.
The autonomy of the local church.
The independence of the local church.
Separation of Church and State.
Baptism of believers only.
Baptism by immersion only.
Priesthood of the believer.
Soul liberty of the individual.

Believing these truths, on Saturday afternoon, December 1, I called on Dr. Robert Hunter, pastor of the Northside Baptist Church. When I mentioned why I was there, he said, "Welcome to the Baptist fold. I knew your Grandfather Parker. He was a good preacher. I knew your six preacher uncles. Son, you are a Baptist by blood."

I said, "No, sir, Dr. Hunter, not by inheritance, but I think I am a Baptist by conviction. But I have some questions. What authority does the convention have over a local church?"

He said, "Absolutely none. The churches do not belong to the convention, but the convention belongs to the churches." That was a cliche I heard often in those days, but I am afraid the de facto situation is the other way around with the convention. Accepting this, however, I told Dr. Hunter I would be interested in joining his church. He said, "Very well, we will have a special service for you."

He called several Mobile pastors and had a special ordination service Sunday afternoon, December 2, 1934; and I became an ordained Baptist preacher after preaching nearly six years as a Methodist.

I suppose there were modernists in strategic places in the convention in those days, but they soft-pedaled their modernism. More and more the liberals came to the fore; so I ceased to support the convention. Later the liberals and neo-orthodoxians were so prominent in the convention that I concluded that I must not support the convention by remaining in it.

In Bed With Flu

Harriette and I went to Pratt City to spend Christmas 1934 with my folks; and while there, we both became ill with flu. We were in bed for three weeks. During this time I received two letters in one mail. One was an offer of a pastorate with an attractive salary and a lovely parsonage.

CHAPTER XIX

Campaigns Continued

We had left Spartanburg, where we had a furnished apartment. But at that time, our home was wherever we laid our heads. We were welcome at my parents' home, but they were having a hard time in the Depression.

Also, I was helping my brother Jimmy and Harriette's sister Julia through Bob Jones College. December is a lean month for an evangelist because there are not many revival meetings held at Christmastime. To have this forced vacation, followed by illness in January necessitating the canceling of two revival meetings, made that bid to a pastorate even more attractive. However, the other letter was from a dear old missionary pastor at Bevier, Kentucky. He said, "You have been recommended to me as an evangelist. We can't offer you anything but a bed." He did not say whether that was in the house. "But," he said, "if you have the missionary spirit, come to us."

After I read those letters, I handed them to Harriette. She read them and handed them back to me. I stuck them under my pillow; and without discussing them, we both fell asleep. When we woke up, she asked me, "Have you decided what we are going to do?" I said, "Yes," and she said, "I know what it is." I asked, "What?" She said, "We are going to Kentucky." I said, "You are mighty right we are. If I don't have the missionary spirit, I am not fit to preach."

I was booked for three two-week campaigns in Michigan from

the middle of March until the middle of May. So in February we went to Bevier, Kentucky.

The Train to Bevier

When we left Birmingham on the train, we were still weak from our three weeks in bed. We transferred at Bowling Green and again at Russell. The little train we rode from Russell to Bevier had only two passenger cars, one for white people and one for black people. The only passengers besides us were four men. They had the train seats turned together and were in a huddle singing filthy songs. We got up and went to the other car.

Two of the men followed us back there and sat in the seat behind us. One of them leaned over and rubbed his arm against my wife's shoulder. I pushed his arm back and said, "Move your arm."

He said to his friend, "Get off of my gun."

I turned around and said, "You don't need a gun. What you need is Jesus Christ."

He asked, "Are you a preacher?"

I said, "I am a Christian and yes, I am a preacher."

He asked, "What are you doing on this train if you are a preacher?"

I said, "I am going to Bevier to hold meetings."

He said, "You are going to Hell."

I said, "No. You are."

He said, "I mean if you are going to Bevier, you are going to Hell. A man got on this train drunk one day and asked the conductor to put him off in Hell. The conductor said, 'All right,' and put him off in Bevier."

When we got to Bevier, I got to thinking that the conductor was almost right about it.

Mr. and Mrs. Wade met us at the train and said, "Hurry and get in the car so there won't be any trouble." A man down the track yelled to several young men and said, "Hey, fellows, another woman has come to town."

That was Saturday evening. We stayed with the Wades. The bed that was promised was in the study. Mr. Wade was a real scholar and had several thousand books. I enjoyed staying in that room and reading a lot of his books.

They had a prayer meeting that Saturday night. About twenty people were there. We got on our knees, and nearly everyone there prayed, "O Lord, please don't let Brother and Sister Parker get killed while they are here." They said there was an average of one murder in Bevier every few weeks and that Cleaton, three miles away, was worse than Bevier. The church was located halfway between Bevier and Cleaton.

One dear old white-haired lady who lived across the street from the church said, "They shot a young man on the church steps Wednesday night. They brought him over to my house, but he was dead before his feet got cold." Somebody said, "Last summer they shot an evangelist out at Nelson, seven miles from here. His wife was at the piano, and the same bullet that killed him went on through and killed her." Harriette was going to play the piano in our meetings. Somebody else said, "Yeah, and they shot at the evangelist who held our meeting last year."

So as they prayed for our safety, all through their prayers you could hear my fervent, "Amen."

We had large crowds in the meetings. The people filled the church, and some stood all the way around the walls of the auditorium. Some roughnecks stayed outside and threw rocks and bricks on the church during the services.

"Hold on There"

One night Pastor and Mrs. Wade and Harriette went to the church ahead of me. I came out of the house and stopped for a moment to pet the Wades' dog, Paul of Iowa. I rolled him over on his back and ran out of the gateway and slammed the gate after myself before the dog could get through. When I was running that short distance, I stuck my hand in my overcoat pocket and took hold of a roll of liberty-head dimes which I had in that pocket to keep them from falling out. As I ran through the gate, a man walked up and pulled a pistol out of a holster and said, "Hold on there."

Before he could get the pistol leveled on me, I swung around with the roll of dimes in my coat and got the drop on the fellow. I said, "Yeah! What do you want?" in a rather confident tone.

He stuck his pistol back in the scabbard and asked, "Is Mr. Fleming at home?"

I said, "You might go down there and see. He is probably at church." He went down the hill toward Mr. Fleming's, and I went down the other side of the hill to the church.

That night during the service somebody pulled the switch in the vestibule of the church, turning out all of the lights. Dear old Pastor Wade, who was seventy-two years of age, went back to turn on the lights; and several fellows took hold of him and threw him on the floor, took his fountain pen and his wallet, and roughed him up a bit. Those fellows came on in the church in the dark.

"God Will Take Care of You"

Pastor Wade got the lights on and came to the platform and told me what had happened. I got up to preach following a solo by Mrs. Wade, "Be not dismayed whate'er betide, God will take care of you," etc. I was both righteously indignant and humanly angry. I lifted the pulpit and set it aside and said, "Some of you yellow scoundrels threw Pastor Wade on the floor and took his fountain pen and his wallet. And some of you good people are praying, 'O God, please don't let Brother Parker get killed.' I want to tell you something. I am not afraid of you cowards. Some of you are going around here with pistols in your pockets. You had better be careful. Those pistols are pointing toward your heels. They may go off and blow your brains out. You can't kill me. I am going to live as long as God lives.

"Oh, you can blow holes in my body and kill me physically, but I will live on in Heaven. But if God strikes you dead, and

He may do that, you will go to Hell and spend eternity.

"Now, aren't you yellow-bellied fellows proud of yourselves for ganging up on a seventy-two-year-old man of God in the dark? May God have mercy on your rotten perverted souls."

I did not know whether I would be shot, but conviction by the Holy Spirit fell on that crowd. When I gave the invitation, people swarmed forward to accept Christ.

Although those meetings were announced for two weeks' duration, we extended them to four weeks; and over seven hundred people were saved. As a result of those meetings, the Baptist Church of Cleaton more than doubled its membership from 250 to more than 500. The last Sunday evening I was in Bevier, Pastor Wade and I sat in his car on a high hill and saw people swarming toward the church at 5:00 P.M. for the 7:30 P.M. service. We hurried to the church, and it was filled, and we started the service at 5:30 P.M.

Michigan

We left Kentucky and went to Michigan for ten weeks of meetings at Adrian, Hamtramck, and Burnside, near Brown City. We had arranged to stop for one night at Bevier on the way from Michigan to Bob Jones College at Cleveland, Tennessee, for Commencement.

They had had services in Bevier every night following our meetings—just singing, praying, and giving testimony. The people said, "The mines are closed temporarily, and one hundred men left on trucks this afternoon to go to Paducah County to pick strawberries, and every man carried a Bible."

One man said, "We used to hear God's name in vain constantly down in the mines. Now we hear His name being praised, and old hymns ringing through the mines."

The Wades wrote the story of their ministry and devoted a whole chapter to our meetings. That chapter was entitled, "The Parker Revival, and Other Revivals" from *Our Life Story* by (Mrs. J. T.) Grace Adelaide Van Duyn Wade and Rev. Joel T.

Wade, B.A., B.D. (Chattanooga, Tennessee: George C. Hudson Company, Publishers, 1954, pp. 547, 548).

Bevier-Cleaton, before we came to make Bevier our home, was reported to be a very tough place, especially Cleaton. It was reported that, at times, when the railroad train was passing through Cleaton that the passenger train had been shot through. It was reported that there had been at least one murder every year, and sometimes more. At one time when I was sick in bed, with an attack of lumbago, Mrs. Wade took my place in leading the church prayer meeting. She, accompanied by a little old lady who lived near, went to the church; and while Mrs. Wade was in the church reading the Scripture lesson of the prayer meeting, a gun was fired just outside of the church. The audience arose, as though they would immediately rush out of the church. Mrs. Wade stopped reading and said, "I think you ladies better sit down," and most of the audience sat down. The reason that she gave this word of caution was because there was only one exit from the room. Then Mrs. Wade led in prayer and went on with the prayer meeting. One of the elders consulted with Mrs. Wade and went out of the church to investigate and came back and reported to her that he saw them carrying a man away. After Mrs. Wade dismissed the prayer meeting, she and the old lady started for the manse; but hearing that the injured man had been taken to the house next to the church, they stopped to see the young man, who had been called out of the prayer meeting, and, without any provocation, was shot by a drunk man, which resulted in his death. Quite a crowd had gathered at this home. Grace prayed for the wounded man and tried to lead him to Christ, and helped in first aid, and then she and the old lady came home.

We discussed the matter of a revival, and decided that nothing short of a month would accomplish what was needed. We knew of the great success of the Bob Jones meetings, and we decided that we would endeavor to get him to hold the meeting. It so happened that he was in England, but I received his reply quite promptly, and he expressed a willingness to come; but when he arrived home in Cleveland, he wrote me that his work was so piled up that his duties were almost killing him, and referred me to John Monroe Parker, and assured me that he would give as good service as he could, that he was the best young preacher that had been educated at his school, and that he felt sure that he and his wife, a splendid pianist, and a good personal worker, would come.

I wrote them, and I promised them a bed and food for a month's time at our home, and sent them the necessary funds to bring them from Birmingham, Alabama, to Bevier.

They came promptly. We held a prayer meeting every morning, a children's meeting every afternoon, and preaching service at night. All three meetings were held in the Presbyterian Church. Parker was everything that we could expect of a preacher, and his wife proved to be a very fine pianist. These services were held each day, a devotional meeting at 10:00 A.M., a children's service at 3:15 P.M. with more than 100 present at these meetings, and evening services at 6:30 P.M. For this service chairs were brought in and placed in the aisles, and all other available space was used to accommodate the large crowds that were present at each and every evening service. Mr. Parker began preaching when he was 19 years of age, and at the time he was with us, he was twenty-five, and he reported that, during these six years, he had missed but five Sundays. Mrs. Parker was also a graduate of Bob Jones College and had majored in piano, and she was a real artist in this line.

Parker and his wife were both well equipped for their work. I was then quite active and led the singing, as I did in all of my meetings. Grace's soprano voice led the women in the choir. During the first two weeks the Christian people were praying, but the Devil was busy during the whole of the first two weeks, and it would seem that but little was being accomplished. But at the end of this two weeks, conviction such as I believe we never saw before became manifest, and from that time, Christians who had been cold were quickened, and souls were saved in great numbers. At the beginning of the third week, the members of the church began to bring in some food, and during the last two weeks of the meeting, my wife and I, as well as the evangelist and his wife, were invited out for meals, and the people showed their interest to the extent that we did not feel that the keeping of the evangelist was any burden to us financially, but their stay with us was a matter for real thanksgiving.

Hardened sinners, who seemed never to have thought on religious matters, were genuinely convicted and converted in great numbers, and the influence of the meeting continued on and on for months, and we think that its influence for good still holds in a marvelous way. The Presbyterian Church was made much stronger, and the Baptist Church received more members than the Presbyterian, and its good effects were still manifest for years, and eternity alone can tell the whole story.

CHAPTER XX

Home in Cleveland, Tennessee

H arriette's little sister was in Bob Jones College; and so that we could continue to help her with her expenses, we had agreed for Harriette to teach piano and organ at the college the academic year 1935-36. Dr. Jones gave us a room in the teachers' wing of the dormitory known as Victory Hall. It was a knotty-pine room which we decorated with rustic things, and this was our home for a year.

Harriette took some special work that summer at the Chadek Conservatory of Music in Chattanooga. I held meetings in Knoxville, Tennessee, and in Georgia and Alabama and recruited a good many students for Bob Jones College.

In the fall I held a countywide meeting in the high school gymnasium at Spindale, North Carolina, sponsored by the Business Men's Evangelistic Club, and had a goodly number of souls. Following that, I held a two-week meeting in the First Baptist Church of Cliffside, North Carolina. We had a large number of professions there.

I returned to Cleveland for a few days and then went back to North Carolina for a short ministry at South Mountain Bible Institute. Mr. Willis Haymaker, who had become the field secretary for the National Association of Business Men's Evangelistic Clubs, went with me.

Sharon, North Carolina

After this, in late October and early November, I held a meet-

ing at Sharon, North Carolina, sponsored by the Billy Sunday
Club of Charlotte. Fred Brown held a meeting simultaneously
at Thrift, North Carolina, under the same sponsorship. Fred and
I were placed in the home of Mr. and Mrs. Frank Graham. Mr.
Graham was an active member of the Billy Sunday Club. The
Sharon Associate Reform Presbyterian Church, which we used
for the campaign, was the Grahams' home church at that time.
The Grahams were wonderful people and were so kind to us boys.
They were greatly concerned about their seventeen-year-old son,
Billy Frank. He had gone forward the previous spring in the
Mordecai Ham campaign and attended meetings which Jimmie
Johnson held in the aftermath of the Ham revival in the
Hawthorne Lane Methodist Protestant Church but did not pro-
fess to be saved. He was a lovable fellow, and Fred and I were
greatly burdened for him. Also, Mr. Prevatt, a good Christian
layman, had a special burden for Billy Frank. One day Mr.
Prevatt came out to the Graham home and asked Fred and me
to pray fervently for Billy Frank. Fred and I knelt by our twin
beds every afternoon and prayed for Billy. He was attending our
meetings alternately.

"Is It Wrong to Dance?"

The second Friday night of the meetings at Sharon, I preached
on "Is It Wrong to Dance?" When I gave the invitation, Billy
Frank came forward along with thirty-seven of his classmates
from Morrison High School. Later he said that he was saved that
night. In fact, in October of 1938 I was in a meeting in the First
Baptist Church of Eustis, Florida. Billy brought Rev. John
Mender, pastor of the Christian and Missionary Alliance Church
in Tampa, 135 miles to ask me to hold a meeting in Tampa.
Billy was the youth pastor there while he was attending Florida
Bible Institute. He said to Mr. Mender in the presence of Pastor
and Mrs. John Hay and Mr. and Mrs. Bunte, in whose home we
were having refreshments, "I want you to hear Monk Parker

preach the sermon he preached the night I was saved on 'Is It Wrong to Dance?' "

In the summer of 1945 I supplied the pulpit at Moody Memorial Church for Dr. Ironside while he was on his vacation. Monday through Friday I preached every day at the noonday service at the Business Men's Service Center down at the Loop. These meetings were begun back in the aftermath of the Moody revival and for many years were broadcast. I was staying down at the Loop at the LaSalle Hotel. Billy Graham happened to be staying there and holding meetings in a tent on the north side of Chicago.

I rode out to his meeting in a street car with him one night. That night he told his life story; and when he told of his conversion, he said it was in the Mordecai Ham meetings. Back down at the Loop he told me that he had already been saved when he came forward in Sharon. "But," he said, "if it were not for you, I would not be in the ministry." This certainly makes it difficult to stand against Billy's neo-evangelicalism, but I must continue to do so.

That night after Billy came forward in Sharon, I signed him up to go to Bob Jones College. He went there in the fall of 1936 but dropped out because of severe sinus headaches. The doctor told him that a warmer climate might help his sinus problem.

My last campaign in 1935 was in the City Hall of Lincolnton, North Carolina.

1936

Zanesville, Ohio, is the city where Dr. Bob Jones had one of his greatest campaigns. Over two thousand joined the churches in one day. That had been about twenty years before; and Dr. A. Stokes Watson, pastor of the large Market Street Baptist Church in Zanesville, wanted him to come back to Zanesville in 1936. Dr. Jones was unable to go, and he sent me a copy of a telegram he sent to Rev. A. Stokes Watson, chairman of the committee representing four Baptist churches in Zanesville. It read as follows:

> Impossible get special letter Parker several days. You can depend on what I tell you. He is man for your meeting. He has been preaching at our college at our Fellowship Convention. He has power and common sense. I recommend him unqualifiedly as best man I know for your purpose.
>
> Bob Jones

Several Bible-believing Baptist churches and the First Congregational Church joined in the sponsorship of the Zanesville meetings of four weeks' duration in the month of January, 1936. Rev. Russell Kauffman, pastor of the Congregational Church, was a gifted singer with a rich baritone voice. He had studied evangelistic songleading under Homer Rodeheaver at Winona Lake. During our campaign Mr. Kauffman decided to become a Baptist. I returned to Zanesville in the fall of 1936 to preach his ordination sermon. It was a special day, Harvest Home Sunday at the Market Street Baptist Church, and the ordination service was held in the afternoon. Russ later led singing for me in several meetings in New York and Pennsylvania. He also traveled for some time with Dr. J. C. Massey of Boston.

Make the Message Plain

One night in the Zanesville campaign as I sat on the platform in front of the alto section of the large chorus choir, I was planning a very profound discourse on a very deep subject. Mr. Kauffman announced the old gospel song, "Christ Receiveth Sinful Men." They came to the chorus, "Make the message clear and plain!" I asked, "Lord, are they singing to me?" They sang the second stanza; and then came the refrain with the altos singing, some of them with rich contralto voices, "Make the message plain, make the message plain!" I preached a simple message on John 3:16; and when I gave the invitation, people came forward in large numbers.

Zanesville, Ohio. (January, 1936)

Sixteen years later I held a meeting in the First Baptist Church of Zanesville, and I met a number of people who told me they were saved the night I preached on John 3:16.

One brilliant young lady who came forward that night was Miss Edwardean Edwards. I got her to go to Bob Jones College, where she served for several years as secretary to Dr. Bob Jones, Jr. She later married Rev. Bob Lang. They had several lovely children who are now graduates of Bob Jones University. Edwardean passed away some years ago.

While in Zanesville, I stayed in the home of a very wealthy elderly widow, Mrs. Bateman, owner of a large glass factory. She was very gracious to me. She bought me a new overcoat, Rolls razor imported from England and made of the finest Sheffield steel, and many other things. She also gave me a nice cash gift plus five hundred dollars for Bob Jones College. She had a Cadillac driven by a chauffeur and also a sports car. She told the chauffeur to see that the sports car was filled with gas and shined spotless each morning for my use.

She insisted on paying Harriette's way on the train to come up and spend some time with me. Harriette got two weeks' leave from the college and spent the last week of that four-week campaign in Zanesville and the first week of a three-week campaign in Franklin, Pennsylvania, where I began meetings on Monday night after closing in Zanesville.

Mrs. Bateman took the Kauffmans and me in her Cadillac to Columbus to meet Harriette, who was coming up from Tennessee. She took us all to the Marimour, a very plush restaurant. She showered Harriette with gifts.

The life of an itinerant preacher is not all "peaches and cream," but it is not all "sticks and stones."

Clear of Debt

I had been in debt since my days in college. With my own college debts and with paying the way of my younger brother and my wife's younger sister in college, I had been hamstrung. But in Zanesville, I got on my knees and told God if He would get me out of debt, I would with His help do my dead level best to stay solvent. The offering in Zanesville was more than enough to clear me of debt. Since then, although there have been times when I could not afford all I wanted, I praise God that there has never been a time when I did not have all I needed. Although at times the situations were very close, and although I have bought things on credit, I thank God that there has never been a time when I could not meet my obligations when due.

Franklin, Pennsylvania

The meetings in Franklin were in a tabernacle seating about three thousand people. It had been built by a businessman, Mr. Lehman, for his prodigy preacher-boy son, Lewis Paul Lehman. Later the Lehmans moved to Wheeling, West Virginia, and had a radio ministry there as well as a tabernacle located on an island in the Ohio River which washed away in a flood. Fourteen years after the meetings in Franklin, I held meetings at Emmanuel Baptist Church in Portland, Oregon, for Dr. Lewis Paul Lehman.

A church was organized in the tabernacle at Franklin. Our crowds were surprisingly large. A tremendous snow came, and the temperature plummeted to 32 degrees below zero. When we walked on the snow, it would make a whistling sound; and "if our eyes we would close, then the lashes froze, until sometimes we couldn't see."

Harriette returned to Bob Jones College after several days in Franklin. I, of course, remained there for three weeks.

Constrained to Go to Mobile

James Zellner was in charge of the Gospel Center in Mobile but had moved it from the ideal location we had to a place where it was difficult to get the people to come. He was trying to revive the work; so he wrote me to come down and preach for him for a few nights. My next campaign was scheduled for Statesville, North Carolina. That campaign was sponsored by the North Carolina Business Men's Evangelistic Clubs and the Statesville Club. They had the cooperation of fourteen good churches and were building a big tabernacle for the meetings.

Although I wanted to spend the time in Cleveland before going to Statesville, I went down to Mobile. The weather was bad, and the meetings were held in an old tent which had several holes in it. Some nights we had pretty fair crowds.

My Brother Lew Saved

One night my brother Lew came into Mobile with his wife and little girl. He was not saved and had asked me not to preach to him. I had told him, "All right, Lew, I won't preach to you; but I will certainly pray for you." That had been seven years, and I had prayed diligently for him every day. He looked in the paper and saw that I was in that meeting. He came and stood outside the tent in the dark and listened. Then it began to rain, and he stepped under the canvas.

Imagine the joy that flooded my soul when he responded to the invitation to accept Christ as his Saviour. After that Lew began to attend church and to live the Christian life until the old bottle tripped him up. At our father's deathbed, he came back to God and lived an exemplary Christian life until he went Home to Heaven twenty-six years later. I had not wanted to go to Mobile, but now I know why I had to go.

Statesville, North Carolina

The Statesville campaign was held in a tabernacle built for that five-week campaign. It was designed by Mr. Willis Haymaker, who had been an advance man for Dr. Bob Jones, and was built so that it could be sawed into sections and re-erected elsewhere. Mr. Don Cochran, who had also been in many of Dr. Jones' big campaigns, led the singing. We had wonderful meetings in Statesville. I preached at Mitchell Women's College and in furniture factories and even in department stores. It would be announced that we would have a brief service; and if anyone wished to leave the store, he was free to go before the service. The doors would be closed. Mr. Cochran would sing, and I would preach a very brief sermon.

Charlotte, North Carolina

In early June I held a two-week campaign at Charlotte in a tabernacle built by the Hawthorne Lane Methodist Protestant Church. Mal Chandler led the music, and we had a great time.

Morganton, North Carolina

Mr. Cochran and Mr. Haymaker had moved the Statesville tabernacle to Morganton, where I was in a three-week meeting. We did not have as much local support in Morganton as we had in Statesville, but we built to a good climax and saw a goodly number of people saved.

Lenoir, North Carolina

Our next meeting was in Lenoir, North Carolina, Mr. Haymaker's home town.

Chester, Pennsylvania

Then we went to Chester, Pennsylvania, for a tent meeting sponsored by the Union Gospel Mission. It was well attended by people from all of the good churches. Mr. George Perry was the director, and he was a wonderful man. Harriette was with me and played the piano. We stayed in the old Crozier Mansion, which had been given to the Billy Sunday Club for a guest home for Christian workers. Mr. and Mrs. Louis Brown were in charge of it. We enjoyed staying in that beautiful mansion with elegant furniture and a large yard of several acres which were a veritable formal garden. The Browns served delicious meals.

I went back and stayed with the Browns some the following year while on the radio in Philadelphia and in meetings in Eastern Pennsylvania.

Hadden Heights, New Jersey

We went from Chester to Hadden Heights, New Jersey, for two weeks of evangelism in the summer tent meetings sponsored by the Hadden Heights Baptist Church. The tent meetings ran all the summer with different speakers each week or two. In 1936, among others, they had Dr. James McGinley, Dr. Bob Ketcham, Dr. Bob Jones, and me. Dr. George Palmer was the pastor, and he had a radio ministry in Philadelphia on WIP from 7:00 to 8:00 each morning and thirty minutes from 10:00 to 10:30 on Tuesday and Thursday mornings. He also ran a bookstore in Philadelphia and had noonday services in the chapel at the bookstore from Monday through Friday. I spoke in all of these services and preached in the tent each night. I also went over to Atlantic City to speak to a large Bible class in the Y.W.C.A.

Philadelphia

Following the meetings with Dr. Palmer, I held a week of meetings in the Gethsemane Presbyterian Church for Moody Holmes. Moody was a fellow student at Bob Jones College; and after his graduation in 1932, he went to Westminster Theological Seminary. Moody took me to meet Dr. J. G. Machan, one of the giants of the faith who left Princeton Theological Seminary to start Westminster with Dr. Robert Dick Wilson, who had passed away. Dr. Antonio Honorio Perpetuo, under whom I studied theology and Hebrew in the graduate school at Bob Jones, had studied those subjects under Dr. Machan and

Dr. Wilson at Princeton, and I had developed reflected admiration for them both.

Pineville, North Carolina

From Philadelphia I drove Harriette to the college, where she was planning to teach, and then went to Pineville, North Carolina, for a tent meeting. Harriette called and said that her sister was getting married and would not be returning to school. She had talked to Dr. Jones, and he had agreed to release her from teaching so that she could join me.

We held meetings that fall in Pineville, North Carolina; Eastport, New York; Franklin, Pennsylvania; and Anniston, Alabama. We saw several hundred souls come to Christ.

We went to Birmingham for Christmas. Dr. Jones called and asked if I would come up to see him and bring Harriette. The head of the piano department had resigned, and he wanted Harriette to take her place at least for the balance of the school year. Since in September Dr. Jones had released her from her contract to teach that year, I agreed. However, I was going to Philadelphia for a radio ministry and evangelistic meetings in the East; so we had an agreement that Harriette could get off for a week or two during the second semester and come to be with me.

Ministry in the East

Beginning January 1, I was on radio station WIP in Philadelphia two days a week; on WIBG, Glenside, Pennsylvania, five days a week; and on WAAT, Jersey City, one day a week. That was before the day of tape recording; so I was on in person. I held meetings at Chester, Pennsylvania; Moresville, New Jersey; Camden, New Jersey; Allentown, Pennsylvania; Doylestown, Pennsylvania; Ogden, Pennsylvania; and in the Church of the Strangers, which is now the Metropolitan Baptist Church, in New York City. This was a great church on 58th

Street, just a block and a half west of Broadway. There were four millionaires in the church, and it was endowed with a fourteen-story apartment house, the church occupying the ground floor, and the parsonage located on the top floor. I was there for a two-week meeting. Homer Rodeheaver led the singing. The pastor, Dr. Spencer, was planning to take a year's leave of absence with a trip around the world. He said to me, "I have talked to the deacons about it, and they agree with my recommendation that you take my place. Now the congregation does not know, but the deacons know that when I return from my trip, I am going to retire." He said, "You have spoken of continuing your graduate work. You could do that here in New York. You could spend a lifetime and would never evangelize everyone in this city block. If you preach Sunday mornings, you can have one of your assistants preach at night, and you can hold evangelistic meetings all around."

Must Do God's Will

This was appealing, but I told him I would need time to pray about it. Dear Dr. Spencer took me to art museums and exotic eating places and points of interest, trying to sell me on New York City. I told him that I did not need to be sold on the opportunity he was offering me, but I would have to know it was God's will for me. I was praying much and seeking God's will about the matter.

Willing to Do His Will

In Philadelphia one cold, cloudy day I was walking up Broad Street going to broadcast. It began to rain, and I stepped into an entrance way of a vacant store building and said, "Lord, if You want me to go to New York, I am willing. If You want me to continue in full-time evangelism, I am willing. But I will tell You what I would like to do. I would like to go back to Bob Jones College as Director of Religious Activities. Dr. Jones has to be away so much of the time. I could teach his class, Practical Instruction for Preachers. I could preach some at chapel and take the Sunday services and teach some Bible. I could counsel students and could direct the athletic program; and when Dr. Jones is on the campus, I could hold revival meetings. And I could continue graduate work."

Dr. Bob Jones, Jr., had not begun to preach at that time. He was Assistant to the President and taught speech and history. A year or two later he turned down a contract with a prominent booking company for scheduling of his famous Shakespearean program, "Curtain Calls," for a solid season at a very lucrative monetary consideration. He wrote the company that he was going to devote that time to preaching the Gospel.

Immediate Answer

Four days after I prayed the above prayer, I received a letter from Dr. Jones inviting me to the college as Director of Religious Activities. Whether it was telepathy, I do not know; but Dr. Jones outlined to me the very job description I had outlined to God.

I did not need to pray about it further. After eight months in the Philadelphia area, I went down to Spartanburg, South Carolina, and held a meeting. Then after a meeting at Brooklyn, Georgia, I went to Bob Jones College at Cleveland, Tennessee, to carry out the duties outlined in Dr. Jones' letter.

CHAPTER XXI

Bob Jones College

I arrived at Bob Jones College in time for the first faculty meeting for the academic year 1937-38. I was to teach General Survey of the Bible, a course to be taken by all of the business college students, and Bible Prophecy, a three-semester-hour course to be taken by college juniors and seniors majoring in Bible. I would be teaching Prophecy and Bible Doctrines in alternate years. Then I would have charge of Dr. Jones' class, Practical Instruction for Preachers, and would teach it in the absence of Dr. Jones. After a couple of years, he turned it over to me to teach regularly. Also, I had charge of the men's athletic department for the first four years I was on the staff. I organized the intramural system and used student assistants to lead the various physical education classes and athletic contests.

All of these athletic events took place after four o'clock in the afternoon.

The hour before chapel each morning, I met with the administrative council. During the war all of my hours until 4:00 P.M. were filled with classes or counseling, and often in the evenings I was busy counseling students. I preached often at chapel and on Sunday mornings, organized the Sunday schools, Mission Prayer Band, Child Evangelism, and the various young people's societies, and approved the prayer leaders for the dormitory prayer groups.

As Director of Religious Activities, I was also responsible for all extension services, sending out faculty members and ministerial students to preach, as well as groups for various kinds of services.

The first year that I taught Prophecy, it was with real trepidation that I undertook the task. In that large class of juniors and seniors, I had such illustrious characters as Tom Malone, Jimmy Mercer, John Gamble, Pat Henry, and George Slater, and sons and daughters of famous prophecy teachers such as Paul Smith and June DeHaan. I stayed up nearly all night almost every night reading everything in the library covering our subject. Then after three weeks of lectures on the book of Isaiah, I gave a test; and on a percentage basis, the highest grade was 25%. I had to scale the grades. I was no longer intimidated by my students. I had learned more than they knew about the book of Isaiah but had failed in teaching them. I had to apply the rules of pedagogy and use a variety of teaching methods. On the next tests which I gave, the grades were altogether satisfactory. The students were learning as well as I. We studied the major and minor prophets, Revelation, and various prophetic themes.

Teaching Load Increased

The second year my teaching load was increased to include Old Testament, taken by all freshmen; and the third year it was increased to include Advanced Old Testament.

Load Continues to Grow

My fifth year on the faculty at Bob Jones followed Pearl Harbor. When a New Testament professor suddenly enlisted as a chaplain just before school opened, I was drafted to take over several of his courses in addition to the teaching load I had. I taught Pauline Epistles, General Epistles, and Johannine Writings. My teaching was supposed to be incidental to my administrative duties.

I mentioned to Dr. Charles Diggery Brokenshire, Dean of the Graduate School, that I needed to review some rules of Greek

Monroe. (1939)

grammar. I had studied one year of classical Greek under Dr. Spangler and a year of Koine Greek under Dr. A. H. Moore and Dr. A. H. Perpetuo; so I had a working knowledge of Greek but needed more. Dr. Brokenshire said, "I would be glad to meet with you one night a week and help you to learn to read your Greek."

"Well," I said, "you are awfully busy, and I am, too."

But he asked, "What night could you meet me?"

I answered, "Tuesday or Thursday nights."

He said, "Very well, I will meet you Tuesday and Thursday nights at seven o'clock in Room 6."

The first night we sat down and had prayer. Then he handed me a copy of Hudleston's *Essentials of New Testament Greek*. He told me to turn to the first page where was given the Greek alphabet and said, "Repeat this after me, please: 'Alpha.' "

I said, "Now, Dr. Brokenshire, I have had a year of classical Greek and some Koine Greek."

He said, "Repeat this after me, please: 'Alpha.' "

I said, "Alpha!"

He said, "Beta."

I repeated.

In periods that followed, he read the entire Greek grammar book to me, stopping after every statement to ask, "Do you understand what that means?" I would answer, "Yes," and he would ask, "What does it mean?" I would tell him, and he would read on. If I said, "I do not understand what it means," he would explain it.

We then read the Epistles and Gospel of John in the Greek. After this he said, "You are now ready for fifth year Greek." Dr. Marshall Neal and I took sixth and seventh year Greek from Dr. Brokenshire. Having read through the entire New Testament in Greek, the seventh year we read in the Septuagint. We had taken Hebrew and were taking German; so we read Amos and Micah in several languages, using a Hexaglot including Latin, which I took in high school; and I had studied a semester of French in college and two years of Spanish in college. We received no credit for German but had to demonstrate a reading knowledge of it in pursuit of the Doctor of Philosophy degree.

Dr. Brokenshire was my major professor in the doctoral program. I accumulated many of my credits by attending a different school each summer for four years. They were Winona Lake School of Theology, Princeton Theological Seminary, Columbia University, and Biblical Theological Seminary in New York City. These schools were liberal; but fortunately, during nine months of the regular academic year, I had wonderful, well-trained teachers, the atmosphere of Bob Jones University, and access to the greatest library on earth from a conservative standpoint.

If I had not been in the business of educating preachers, I would not have submitted myself to these pressures, although their liberalism to me was like pouring water on a duck's back. I had seen the Gospel work too long. Besides, I preached every weekend. One of my professors at Princeton in the summer of 1945 could hardly believe it when I told him that I preached one Sunday at Tremont Temple Baptist Church, Boston; the next Sunday at Grace Chapel, Upper Darby, Pennsylvania; the next Sunday at Churchill Tabernacle, Buffalo; and the next Sunday at Moody Church, Chicago.

Watching Satan Bait His Traps

I had a unique opportunity, despite the perils of theological pitfalls, to witness Satan set and bait his traps. It was in a day when modernism was wearing out, and its exponents were confessing their folly.

Fosdick had written in his book, *Successful Christian Living*: "The Modernistic movement has watered down the thought of the divine, and may we be forgiven for this, left souls standing like the ancient Athenians before an altar to the Unknown God" (p. 163).

Many liberals, realizing the failure of modernism, turned to neo-orthodoxy, which is as "the same old wolf in a new suit of sheepskin." Neo-orthodoxy is dishonest. The neo-orthodoxian uses orthodox terms while holding the old modernistic views.

The liberals decided that they needed the evangelicals.

The late Dr. John MacKay, who was then president of Princeton Theological Seminary, returned from Amsterdam in the summer of 1945 after having helped to set up the World Council of Churches, which was to organize there later. He was elated over the response from many denominations.

"A New Evangelicalism"

The faculty and students of Princeton were assembled in front of Miller Hall and sat on the lawn as Dr. MacKay spoke on the ecumenical movement. He thought that evangelicals could be brought into it and that it would be a good thing but that there would need to be a New Evangelicalism.

A year later Dr. Harold John Ockenga, who was at the time the president of the new seminary founded by Charles Fuller, had a formula for that New Evangelicalism and later was under the impression that he coined the term.

I wrote my Ph.D. dissertation on "The Old Testament Revelation of the Future Life with Special Attention to its Consistency in All Periods." My major subject was Old Testament, and my two minors were Theology and New Testament. However, my principal field of service has been administration and evangelism.

Harriette attended summer school at Cincinnati Conservatory of Music four summers and earned the Master of Music degree. Following that, she attended the American Conservatory of Music in Chicago the summers of 1943/1944 and U.C.L.A. the summer of 1945. Although she took organ lessons from some distinguished organists, much of her work was in composition. She was concerned over the need of good Christian music and did compose some which unfortunately was never published. In 1946, the summer I studied at Columbia University, she was with me in New York. We had apartments with the Bob Shapers and the Herbert Hoovers, who were studying in New York. The Hoovers traveled with us in evangelistic work several years, and Herbert led the singing. In those days I think he was the best gospel soloist in the country.

While Harriette loved her work at Bob Jones College, where she was coordinator of the Music Department and Director of the Church Choir, her greatest love in music was in evangelism. She looked forward to the time when we would go back into full-time evangelism.

I, too, felt that desire; but I also felt that I should remain at Bob Jones during those crisis years of the school: war years, aftermath of the war years, and years of expansion into a university.

In addition to being Director of Religious Activities and teacher of Practical Instruction for Preachers, I had been made Assistant to the Acting President, Dr. Bob Jones, Jr. When we expanded into a university and moved to Greenville, he became President, and I was Assistant to the President.

Before leaving for the Christmas holidays in 1946, I preached a series of sermons for the radio on records to be played daily while I was away. Three of them were on Romans 8:26-28.

We went down to Montgomery, where I conducted the funeral of Mrs. Bob Jones, Sr.'s, mother, Mrs. Estelle Stollenwerck, whose husband was a cousin of Harriette's father.

Harriette had a cousin there about her own age who had married a man more than fifteen years her senior. We had breakfast with them. When we went to our room in the Thomas Jefferson Hotel, Harriette asked, "When I die, are you going to marry a girl fifteen years younger than you?"

I answered, "No."

She then asked, "Are you going to marry a widow?"

I answered, "No."

She persisted, "Are you going to marry an old maid?"

Again I said, "No."

Then she asked, "Whom will you marry?"

I said, "I will just keep you."

I believe she had a premonition she was going to die. She said, "I believe in second marriages; and if I die, you will need a wife. Marjorie Parker is the one for you."

Harriette and Marjorie were classmates, and Harriette dearly loved Marjorie. Since Marjorie and I were both on the administrative staff and had a lot of business together, and since we had the same name, I had a sort of brotherly feeling for her, but I was a married man, and there was no romance in our relation to each other. We were friends.

Harriette knew this, too, but she had a premonition of death which manifested itself several times in the few days that followed.

After the funeral of Mrs. Jones' mother, on our way to Birmingham, where we spent Christmas with my parents and where I held a four-day meeting beginning Thursday night, December 26, in the Birmingham Gospel Tabernacle, she said, "I like the way you conducted the funeral. When I die, I want my funeral conducted just like that."

Later she said, "Funeral homes are so well arranged for funerals. I want my funeral in a funeral home." I said, "Honey, will you please quit talking about dying."

We had a wonderful meeting in Birmingham. Dr. Glenn Tingley, the pastor, owned a radio station; and nearly every fundamental preacher in North Alabama had a program on that station. On Sunday afternoon, December 29, in the Birmingham City Auditorium, we had a great rally sponsored by all of the churches on that station, and we filled that mammoth coliseum which seated about eight thousand people. I preached a salvation message, and many were saved. As a result, the tabernacle which seated about twelve hundred was filled that night. I preached on "Hell," and many were saved.

CHAPTER XXII

From Sunshine Into Dark Shadows

The next morning we left Birmingham "on cloud nine," as the saying goes. This was December 30, 1946, and I was driving a 1937 De Sota, which I had driven all during the war, but it was still in good condition.

We were going over to Greenville, South Carolina, to see the university buildings which were under construction and to take a little holiday trip. As we drove down 20th Street, we passed the Luquire Brown Funeral Home. Harriette turned and looked back and asked, "Was that a funeral home?"

I said, "Yes."

She said, "Don't forget. I want my funeral in a funeral home."

An hour later a young man who had picked up a hitchhiking woman and, according to what the highway policeman told me, had his hands on her body while she held the steering wheel of his car, plunged across the highway, striking my car fifty-seven inches on my side of the white line in the center of the highway, causing us to veer across the highway. An oncoming truck with its horn sounding over and over kept coming on. We stopped on the shoulder on our left of the highway to keep from going over a deep bluff. The truck turned into us on Harriette's side of the car. I thought the driver would turn to his left as he had time and room to do so. The two vehicles that struck us had raced all the way from Atlanta, according to a man who stopped at the scene. Harriette was rendered unconscious and tarried fourteen hours.

A little after 2:00 A.M. from a hospital in Birmingham, Harriette went to be with the Saviour she loved so well and served so beautifully.

Harriette was not only a talented musician; she was deeply spiritual but not super pious in her manner. She was nearly always cheerful and was a blessing to all who knew her.

Below is a tribute paid to her recently in an article in *Faith for the Family* by Mrs. Lefty Johnson, quoting Dr. Bob Jones, Jr., who preached Harriette's funeral at a funeral home in Birmingham.

> The music for "University Hymn" was composed by Harriette Stollenwerck Parker, one of the early graduates of Bob Jones College in Florida, who for many years served her alma mater as a member of the music faculty. Dr. Jones says of this gifted woman: "Harriette was one of the most godly, sweet-spirited, and cheerful Christians I have ever known. She was also beautiful. I especially remember the lovely pianologues she used to give at Bible Conference and vespers. She would sit at the piano and play a melody while reciting the words of a great hymn. My favorite was 'God Leads His Dear Children Along.' "
>
> Of Mrs. Parker's death Dr. Jones says: "Harriette was killed in an automobile accident about the last day of the year preceding our move to Greenville, South Carolina. Interestingly enough, my grandmother had been buried the day before Christmas, and Harriette's husband, Dr. Monroe Parker, had conducted the funeral. Harriette was the youngest person present. A week later, to the day, I conducted Harriette's funeral in Birmingham, Alabama. She and her husband had decided to visit Greenville to look over the new campus and buildings that were under construction. On the way they collided with a heavy truck, and Harriette was killed. To me Harriette's death closed an era in the life of this institution. Though on earth she never knew Bob Jones College as a university, no one would delight more in the blessing of God upon the school these thirty years since the Lord called her home."

I Wanted to Die

When Harriette died, I felt as if I wanted to die also. However, my brother James, who had come from his home in Texas to the funeral, drove me back to Bob Jones College. My left leg was in a cast because my knee was broken in the wreck; and there were other injuries, and I was in no condition to ride a train or a bus.

Jim turned on his radio to the Cleveland station, and there I was preaching and saying, "And we know that all things work together for good to them that love God, to them who are the called according to his purpose" (Rom. 8:28).

God was very near and dear to me in the months that followed. In those lonely nights I completed my dissertation on the afterlife, defended it before the faculty of the Graduate School of Religion, and received my Ph.D. diploma from the hand of Dr. Bob Jones, Sr.

I Wanted to Live

I was God's servant and wanted to live. My summer was filled with a fabulous schedule of evangelistic campaigns.

Very often I would think of getting married again, but marrying a woman of Harriette's equal would be impossible unless, unless I should take her suggestion: "Marjorie Parker is the one for you." The more I thought, the more my head agreed with this; but I needed to wait on my heart. Then one night right after supper I saw Marjorie coming out of the dining hall, and suddenly my heart agreed with my head. I realized that I was in love with her. We read in Genesis 2:18, "And the Lord God said, It is not good that man should be alone; I will make him an help meet for him."

He certainly gave me an "help" meet for me. When we were in college, Marjorie was elected the most popular girl. When she was a sophomore, she became secretary to Dr. Bob Jones, Sr., and office manager. Many a young swain hung around that office as much as he was allowed to.

In college she was president of Sigma Kappa Rho Literary Society, vice-president of the Pan-Hellenic Council, vice-president of the Epworth League, editor-in-chief of the *San Andros Staff,* the college annual, and secretary of the student body, and many other things. She was elected the Best All-Around Girl in college. She certainly deserved that distinction. After her graduation, she took graduate work in speech and coordinated the weekly vesper programs and planned and directed one out of every four of them.

She and some of the other young ladies on the staff used to go horseback riding wearing smart-looking habits. She played golf and tennis and took flying lessons, but I grounded her when we got married. I have often felt that God saved her for me by making her Dr. Jones' secretary and placing her under that tremendous responsibility. Dr. Jones gave her up as his secretary and asked her to find her successor. She selected Arlene Carlson. Marjorie was made coordinator of freshman speech, with some twelve teachers in her department, and director of dramatic production.

We were married by Dr. Bob Jones, Sr., in his home on January 5, 1948. Present were Dr. and Mrs. Jones, Dr. and Mrs. Bob Jones, Jr., Dr. Grace Haight, Miss Hazel Claire Riley, my brother Lew's daughter, Jo Ann, who was a student in Bob Jones Academy, Marjorie's sister Mary and her husband, Bob Lindsay, who came from Columbia, Tennessee, to attend our wedding, and Guyla Pearson, Dr. Bob Jones, Jr.'s, secretary and coworker with Marjorie in the administrative offices. Mrs. Jones served a beautiful and delicious wedding supper. Then Marjorie and I slipped away for our honeymoon in Columbia, South Carolina; Savannah, Georgia; Tallahassee, Waukulah Springs, and Panama City, Florida; and Dothan, Alabama. On the way back to Greenville, we shopped in Atlanta.

In the early spring I held a meeting at the First Baptist Church of North Charleston. Marjorie went with me, and we enjoyed the beautiful gardens as well as the historic sites of this quaint old city. I have held several campaigns in Charleston in later years.

The summer of 1948 was the first summer Marjorie traveled

My second wife, Marjorie. We were married
January 5, 1948

with me in evangelistic work. We held a meeting in South Texas; then a series of meetings in Pennsylvania; then a youth conference at Wolf Lake, Michigan; a camp meeting at Brandywine, Pennsylvania; then a week of one-night services in New York State.

One Friday night I spoke at Fairhaven, New York, on the southern shore of Lake Ontario. I was to preach the following night at the Rochester Youth for Christ. In 1948 Youth for Christ had not embraced neo-evangelicalism. I looked at the map and discovered that Fairhaven was not very far from Rochester; so we decided to go on over there after the service on Friday night. We checked in at the Sheraton Hotel in Rochester and slept most of Saturday.

The plan was for me to leave Marjorie in Rochester and take a pullman train to New York City Saturday night after Youth for Christ, where I was to supply the pulpit for Dr. William Ward Ayer on Sunday while he was on vacation. Then I would take a train back to Rochester on Monday, and we would drive to Boston, where I was to speak at the Bob Jones Alumni Banquet on Tuesday night.

Late Saturday afternoon Marjorie said, "If you feel like driving all night, I will go on to New York City with you after Youth for Christ tonight." So we started out. This was before the thruway was completed, and we went down and started east on Highway 20. We were about the only people traveling that night. At about 1:00 A.M. we stopped for gas thirty-five miles south of Syracuse. When we started to go on, I discovered that the battery was dead. The generator was burned out. There would not be a bus to New York that night along that route, and there seemed to be no traffic. Dr. William Ward Ayer was away on his vacation, and I felt that I had to get to New York; so we took it to the Lord in prayer.

A man and his wife had come down from Syracuse to spend the weekend with her parents there at that little service station and crossroads store. When I told him my plight, he said, "We live in Syracuse. We will go back home and come down here next weekend, and we will take you to Syracuse where you can get a train for New York City."

We left our car at the service station, and that dear couple, Mr. and Mrs. Francisco, took us to Syracuse. They were Catholics, and we led them to Christ. We got to the New York Central Railway Station just in time to get our tickets for New York and were able to get a lower berth, the only vacant berth on the train. We pulled into Grand Central Station at 10:20 A.M., caught a cab and went to the Salisbury Hotel, where we had a reservation. I took a shower and dressed and walked onto the platform at Calvary Baptist Church at exactly 11:00 A.M. Dr. Ralph Mitchell, Dr. Ayer's assistant, shook hands with me and said, "Hello, Dr. Parker. Did you have a good night's sleep?" I answered, "Fine."

We certainly had a delightful nap that Sunday afternoon. On Monday I flew to Syracuse, purchased a generator, took a bus down to where I left my car, had a mechanic to put it in, and drove back to New York to get Marjorie, arriving at the Salisbury Hotel in the early evening.

Tuesday we drove to Boston, where we had the banquet at the Bradford Hotel. The next day we drove to Ogunquit, Maine. Then we returned to New York, driving through New Hampshire and Vermont. The following Sunday I preached at the Temple Baptist Church in Brooklyn.

Of course, I preached the Lord Jesus Christ everywhere, and we had many saved.

In the fall of 1948 nearly every mail brought invitations for evangelistic meetings. I gave serious consideration to returning to full-time evangelism. I had found it necessary to cancel several engagements because of the preponderance of my work at the university. Dr. Jones was wonderful to me and allowed me to go hold meetings when my work would permit it. However, the time came when I would have to curtail my evangelistic work greatly to do work I felt that others could do as well as, if not better, than I. So in the spring of 1949 I resigned to return to full-time evangelistic work.

CHAPTER XXIII

Back in Full-Time Evangelism

We purchased a home in Greenville near the university. In the next five years and three months, I held 108 campaigns, 25 of them cooperative—that is, with groups of Bible-believing churches—and 83 of them single-church meetings.

We moved from a little apartment on the campus in April, 1949, about three months before school was out. We expected our first child to be born in June. I went for a campaign to Miami with four churches in a circus tent borrowed from Ringling Brothers.

I was there two weeks and expected the baby to come the next week while I was at home. We waited a week; then I went to Princeton, Indiana, for a campaign in a tent 100 feet x 120 feet, located on the Gibson County fairgrounds. The meeting was sponsored by Christian laymen. Over fifty churches canceled their Sunday night services, and we had tremendous crowds with many people saved. I was there for two weeks and returned home, feeling that surely the baby would be born while I was at home that week, but that hope was in vain.

My First-Born When I Was Forty

I went next for a two-week camp meeting at Mount Olivet, Pennsylvania. It was the second Monday, August 9, 1949, when our good friend, Mrs. Elizabeth Edwards, called to tell me that

Marjorie was doing well in the hospital and that I was the father of John Monroe, Jr.

It was not easy to stay through the meeting which closed the following Sunday night, and I drove through the night in the rain for many miles on slick black asphalt roads to get home as early as possible. We had arranged for a practical nurse, a specialist, to take care of Marjorie and the baby and the house, food, et al, until I returned home.

We engaged her again two and a half years later when our other child was born, March 25, 1952. I was with Marjorie for that blessed event. God gave us a girl this time, and we named her Penelope Anne for my Grandmother Josephine Penelope Adams Moseley and Marjorie's sister, Anne. We call her Penny.

When John was two weeks old, I held a short series of meetings at the Crossroads Baptist Church near Greenville and was able to stay at home. On John's second Sunday in this world, we took him to church in a bassinet. The following Sunday I began a two-week meeting in Columbia, South Carolina, in Eau Claire Baptist Church and took Marjorie and the baby, and from that time they traveled with me to most of the meetings except for a short time before and after Penny was born. When Penny joined us, I took them all.

We had a great meeting at Columbia. One night we sang fifty-six stanzas of invitation songs with people coming forward on every stanza.

In September of 1949 I held a three-week campaign in the First Baptist Church, Peekskill, New York, with Dr. Gordon Ham, pastor. Evangelist Vincent Cervera led the singing. He was a good singer and trumpeter and an excellent platform man. The pastor of the First Baptist Church of Tarrytown, the old home church of the John D. Rockefeller, Sr.'s, wanted me for meetings and invited me for a special Wednesday night service.

I went home from Peekskill and got Marjorie and John, and we took out for New York since I was going from Tarrytown on over to Buffalo to start a campaign the following Sunday.

In Tarrytown we stayed in the old Rockefeller mansion, which was at that time the parsonage for the First Baptist Church. It was furnished with ornate though beautiful furniture. We took a dresser drawer out of a bird's-eye maple dresser and placed it on the marble top of the dresser, put a pillow in the deep drawer, and made a bed for John.

After that he slept in dresser drawers all over the country. Since we had a couple of nights before going to Buffalo, we went by Schenectady, where Dr. Bob Jones, Sr., was in meetings. We stayed at the Sheraton Hotel, where John again slept in a dresser drawer. Dr. Jones came up to our room after breakfast the next morning; and when he saw John in his drawer, he asked, "Why have you got him in a casket?" He talked to John, and John cooed and bubbled and jabbered at Dr. Bob.

Dr. Bob Jones, Sr., holding John
when he was three weeks old.

When Penny was a baby, she also slept in dresser drawers in many hotels.

In September of 1952 I was in a campaign in Evansville,

Indiana. The day before we closed on a Sunday night, Marjorie flew home with Penny, who was six months old. I kept John with me and brought him home by car. From the time he was two years old, John always sat on the front seat and seemed to be listening to every word I said. That Saturday night he got up and stood in front of the pulpit. I stopped preaching and asked, "What is it, John?"

He said, "I have got chewing gum in my hair."

A dear lady came to the rescue.

When Marjorie arrived, she called to tell me she had arrived home safely and to give me a report on my mail. In five years and three months, I held twenty-five cooperative campaigns with a plurality of non-ecumenical churches and eighty-three single-church campaigns. In all of these engagements I had only one cancellation. Marjorie reported, "Your meeting at Liberty, North Carolina, that was to start two weeks from tomorrow has been canceled."

My children
John and
Penny

I said, "Good, I will come home. I have turned down numbers of invitations for this fall, but it is too late to book anything else."

Marjorie said, "Something else will open."

I hung up the phone and it rang again. I picked it up, and it was Pastor Gobbel Phillips inviting me for meetings at Grace Baptist Church, Decatur, Alabama. I said, "Brother Phillips, I don't know Grace Baptist Church. I held a citywide meeting in Decatur in 1941 before neo-evangelicalism entered the arena."

He said, "Well, they know you. They are the friends of Dr. John Cowell, who withdrew from Central Baptist Church, and Grace Baptist Church is independent."

"Then," I said, "I will come if you can take me beginning two weeks from tomorrow."

We had wonderful meetings. However, Brother Phillips had come from a Southern Baptist church and was not happy with the independent status of the church. I told him that he ought to jump up and clap his heels together because his church was not in ecclesiastical bondage and affiliation with liberal colleges and seminaries. Some of the deacons remembered this two years later when Brother Phillips left the church on account of illness.

The chairman of the pulpit committee called and asked me if I would consider the pastorate. My answer was, "No, I am an evangelist and am booked for more than a year ahead." Then he asked if I would come and preach for them. I was planning to go home and be at the Bob Jones University board meeting and remain during the Commencement exercises; so I had that Sunday open. I agreed.

Neo-evangelicalism had just begun to infiltrate the cooperative campaigns, and evangelists that I never dreamed would compromise were yielding to the pressure.

Neo-evangelicalism

One evangelist who had enjoyed great success in meetings with fundamentalists only said to me: "I saw that Billy Graham has the National Association of Evangelicals behind him. He has that spot. But I want to preach to as many people as I can; so I said, "Where are the big crowds? They are in the Southern Baptist Convention." So I went down to Atlanta and joined the First Baptist Church. It has opened associationwide meetings to me."

I asked, "Can you support the Southern Baptist Convention with its liberal theological seminaries and colleges, its liberal Sunday school literature, etc.?"

He said, "Yes, it helps my ministry, and my ministry is the most important thing in the world to me."

I answered, "The cause of Jesus Christ is more important to me than my ministry. I want my ministry to contribute to that."

The pulpit committee at Decatur said, "We want an evangelist. You can be away for meetings if you will line up proper substitutes while you are away." After much prayer I answered a unanimous call to Grace Baptist Church, Decatur, Alabama. While there I held ten campaigns a year and brought in proper supply preachers, paying their expenses and their honorariums myself.

My first Sunday in the pastorate was August 9, 1954, and we had only 170 in Sunday school. The Sunday I read my resignation to accede to my election as President of Pillsbury Conservative Baptist Bible College, Owatonna, Minnesota, we had 451 in Sunday school.

God not only gave a wonderful ministry at Grace Baptist for three years and five months but also enabled us to bring together twelve churches and form the Conservative Baptist Association of Alabama. The Conservative Baptist Association of America was a fine organization until certain neo-evangelicals infiltrated it and took the leadership of it. When that happened, we pulled Pillsbury College out of it, along with about three hundred churches. The Conservative Baptist Association of Alabama dissolved. Working together during the time I was in Decatur, however, we built Christian Dells Bible Conference and had wonderful fellowship. Christian Dells still flourishes with the cooperation of some of those churches and other independent Baptist churches.

The summer of 1956 I was the main speaker at the Minnesota Baptist Convention during Family Week at Medicine Lake. That fall I held an eight-day meeting at Fourth Baptist Church in Minneapolis, Dr. Richard V. Clearwaters, pastor. In November of that year I was the main speaker for the Central Regional of the Conservative Baptist Association of America at Eau Claire, Wisconsin.

CHAPTER XXIV

Citadel of Fundamentalism

U nder the long-time leadership of the great fundamentalist, Dr. William Bell Riley, the Minnesota Baptist Convention was known as the citadel of fundamentalism. This state
convention had pulled out of the American (Northern) Baptist
Convention in 1957 because of modernism in the denominational
theological seminaries and missionary program, plus an action
to determine the number of voting messengers a local church
could have in the American Baptist Convention by the amount
of money given by the church to the unified budget of the
convention.

This action occasioned the formation of the Conservative Baptist Association.

Pillsbury was under the patronage of the Minnesota Baptist
Convention, now renamed Minnesota Baptist Association and
composed of independent churches. Pillsbury had flourished
since 1854, first as a college and then as the Minnesota Baptist
Academy, until the late George Pillsbury and his wife, Margaret,
had built four fine buildings on the campus and endowed the
school with a quarter of a million dollars. That was in 1886, and
the name was changed to Pillsbury Academy. In 1921 it became
a military prep school. All of this time the institution was under
the patronage of the Minnesota Baptist Convention, which
elected the directors.

When a great contender for the faith, Dr. R. V. Clearwaters,
was elected to the board and became chairman, they closed the

Academy, which had become liberal, and opened a Bible college. Dr. Clearwaters, whose hands were full with a great church and a theological seminary, was asked to be the president but declined. He agreed to serve in the interim until the board could find a president.

In November of 1957, the first semester of Pillsbury as a Bible College, I was elected as president. I flew up to meet the Presidential Committee and to look over the college. Northwestern had closed the Seminary and Bible College but not the Liberal Arts College. So the Bible teachers and Christian Education teachers, most of whom came to Northwestern under Billy Graham's tenure, had been brought to Owatonna as the first faculty of Pillsbury.

Penny, Marjorie, Monroe, John. Pillsbury College.

Since we had a diverse philosophy of education, the faculty resigned; and we had a one hundred percent turnover in full-time faculty at the end of the first year. The board stood behind me. I had insisted that the president must have authority to employ and dismiss faculty, control finances within an approved budget, and in general run the college. It was delegated authority, and the board could fire the president if he did not run the college to suit them. The authority delegated to me caused the resignation of the faculty; and when the board voted with a big majority to accept their resignation, a campaign to overthrow the board ensued. A meeting of the fifty-seven-person board of the Minnesota Baptist Convention was called at the request of the faculty; and that board which was elected by the same convention that elected the college board and had no authority over it voted to censure the college board by a majority of one.

The opposition subsided when we opened school for the second year with a thirty percent increase in the student body.

At the 1959 annual meeting of the Minnesota Baptist Convention, I was elected president of the convention and served in that position four years, being re-elected three times. There was a bit of satisfaction but no bitterness in presiding over the board that had censured the Pillsbury board.

In the seven years and eight months that I was president of Pillsbury under the hand of God, we acquired seven buildings, remodeled two of the old buildings, and enhanced the property over a million and a half dollars, while the Certified Public Accountant's reports showed a profit from operation each year. We also showed more than a six hundred percent increase in the student body in seven years.

I felt that God had taken me to Pillsbury for a special job for which He had uniquely prepared me and that my work there was finished. So on April 27, 1965, I read the following statement at the college chapel service:

> Pillsbury College has a continuity going back 111 years. Prior to 1957 it was a military academy. When my beloved friend and God's servant, Dr. R. V. Clearwaters, became

Chairman of the Board, the Academy was changed to a Bible College. God has blessed the college as few institutions have been blessed.

In February 1958 the Lord led me to the college to make a contribution for which He had peculiarly equipped me through years of experience in evangelism and in the administration of Bob Jones University, where I was a student in Florida and a member of the administration in Tennessee and South Carolina.

I am thankful that I could make a contribution during the formative years of Pillsbury Baptist Bible College, and I rejoice in the opportunity that has been mine to help in this way.

Wonderful and glorious have been the achievements in the lives of hundreds of young people who have entered these halls. Clear and forceful has been the testimony that has gone out from this fortress of truth. Firm the foundation that has been laid. To God be the glory, great things He hath done!

If Jesus tarries, I expect to rejoice in years to come over the great institution I expect to see reared over this foundation; and I do now rejoice over the hundreds of young people who have already received their training here as they go on to greater achievements for God around the world. My love and prayers will follow each of you as you go on to serve our Lord through the years.

I have had a growing conviction that my work as President of Pillsbury College should cease soon after the next academic year is launched. The work God brought me here to do is just about finished. Consequently, I have submitted my resignation as President of Pillsbury College to the Board of Trustees. I shall support the school and pray for her greater glory.

I am grateful to God for the prayers and gifts of thousands who have helped in this task and pray that such cooperation with my successor may continue with ever-increasing momentum.

> **Arise, ye sons and daughters,**
> **Pillsbury's warriors all!**
> **From jungles far away,**
> **From the town and hamlet small**
> **Come cries of souls sinbound**

And doomed to endless woe.
All your hearts with love aflame
Arise and to them go!

The following resolution was passed by the Pillsbury Board of Trustees:

Whereas, Dr. Parker has tendered his resignation to the Trustee Board of Pillsbury Baptist Bible College effective August 31, 1965;

And, whereas the Trustee Board voted unanimously to ask him to reconsider his resignation and to continue the wonderful work he has done in our college, which he declined;

Therefore, be it resolved, that we express our deep appreciation to Dr. and Mrs. Parker for their faithful, unselfish devotion to Pillsbury College for seven and one-half fruitful years;

Be it further resolved that we will pray God's richest blessing upon Dr. Parker as he continues in the field of evangelism.

CHAPTER XXV

Report to the Board

Below is the report I gave to the Board of Trustees of Pillsbury at the end of the academic year, 1964-65, typical of the eight annual reports God enabled me to give:

PILLSBURY BAPTIST BIBLE COLLEGE,
OWATONNA, MINNESOTA

ANNUAL REPORT OF THE PRESIDENT FOR 1964-65

On Thursday night, May 27, 1965, we brought to a close the eighth academic year of PILLSBURY BAPTIST BIBLE COLLEGE. It is the expressed opinion of the officers of Administration, the faculty, and many patrons that this marked the end of the most fruitful year to date from the standpoint of achievement in the lives of the students in general.

Below is a list of the young people who graduated from the various levels of the institution and a statement of the course each plans for the future:

1. Dorothy Allen—Married to James Freerksen, a Central Seminary student and Pillsbury alumnus.
2. Tony Angus—Further teacher training.
3. Charles Baker—San Francisco Conservative Baptist Theological Seminary.
4. William Bardwell—Central Seminary.
5. Charles Benson—Central Seminary.
6. James Bliss—Teaching—Westminster Academy, Glendale, California.
7. Charles Browne—Central Seminary.
8. Gene Brush—Central Seminary.

Dr. Bob Jones, Jr., and Dr. Parker at the
Minnesota Baptist Convention.

Dr. and Mrs. Clearwaters with the Parkers.

Revivals, Pillsbury days.

**Strolling with Dr. Rammel at the 25th Anniversary
of Pillsbury College.**

Monroe Parker and Richard Clearwaters.

9. Neil Cadwell—Pastorate, Maderson, Wyoming.
10. Helen Caffey—Teaching—Silver State Baptist Academy, Denver, Colorado.
11. Robert Crummett—Youth Pastor.
12. Paul Ferris—Trinity Seminary.
13. Sherrie Gerard—Mankato State Teachers College.
14. John Gilmore—Tennessee Temple Seminary.
15. Grace Goodman—Married to a Pillsbury senior.
16. Evelyn Gorse—Mankato State Teachers College.
17. Haido Hionidou—Married.
18. Conrad Jorgenson—Pillsbury College Staff.
19. Jerry Longstreth—Tennessee Temple Seminary.
20. Nancy McCurdy—Married to ministerial student.
21. James McDougal—Central Seminary.
22. James Maring—Counseling youth—Arizona Baptist.
23. Douglas Neumann—Central Seminary.
24. Charles Nichols—Central Seminary.
25. Judy Petersen—Engaged to Pillsbury senior. Will work and wait.
26. Kelsey Pietsch—San Francisco Conservative Baptist Theological Seminary.
27. Judy Pratt—Mankato State Teachers College.
28. Diane Ramage—Teaching—Pensacola, Florida, Christian School.
29. Ronald Robinson—Indefinite.
30. Genevieve Schoepf—Pillsbury Graduate School.
31. James Seward—Central Seminary.
32. Joann Shumway—Has applied to WCBM
33. Jack Smith—Mankato State Teachers College.
34. Anna Sowers—Engaged to Central Seminary student.
35. Marilyn Steffek—Teaching—Pillsbury College.
36. Charles Surrett—Central Seminary.
37. Rosanne Van Pelt—Is now Mrs. Charles Surrett.
38. Gerald Webber—Central Seminary.
39. Curly Werth—Working—Central Seminary extension.
40. William Wickham—Pastorate.

The degree of Master of Arts:

1. Miss Grace Bauer—Secretary of Admissions, Pillsbury College.
2. Mr. Don Nelson—Youth Pastor, Fourth Baptist Church.

Two-Year Diplomas:

1. William Davis—Working in Owatonna.
2. Mary Edwards.
3. Jan Hart—Married to Charles Baker.
4. Linda Smith—Wife of Jack Smith.
5. Kathy Webber—Wife of Gerald Webber.

The work of the college in general has progressed wonderfully under "the good hand of our God." In the two semesters we matriculated 450 students, 420 of whom were full-time students.

The faculty as a whole has rendered faithful, efficient and loyal service. Where there have been exceptions, admonition has been given and corrections have been made.

All of last year's faculty have returned for the 1965-66 academic year with the exception of the writer and his wife, Mr. and Mrs. Douglas Caffey, and Mr. and Mrs. Lawrence Dickerson. The superb work of Mr. Caffey as Dean of Students is appreciated by this administration, and, of course, the fine work of the others is also appreciated.

A splendid faculty for this year has been organized, including the following new members:

B. Myron Cedarholm, B.A., B.D., Th.M., D.D., LL.D.
Thelma Cedarholm, B.A., M.R.E., Litt.D.
Max Foster, B.S.
Don Scoville, B.M.E., M.M.E.
Mrs. Don Scoville.
Marilyn Steffek, B.A.
Richard Weeks, B.A., M.A., B.D., Th.M., D.D.
Marilynne June Weeks

During the last year Mr. Joel Kettenring has received the Th.M. degree from Central Seminary. Several other faculty members are working on degrees.

The prospects for student enrollment for 1965-66 are very good. Unless we have more cancellations and "no shows" than usual, we will have approximately 400 dormitory students and some 43 married students. This will denote an increase of approximately 30 over the enrollment the first semester last year. The average annual increase for the last seven years has been 51 (from 93 to 450), figured on a two-semester, annual basis. The indications are that this increase will be sustained.

We have edited and sent out PILLSBURY BULLETINS to a wide constituency. The letters that pour into our office daily indicate that the editorials have strengthened the position of the institution in the hearts and minds of Bible-believing people.

As I have stated in other reports, it is easy to over-advertise and easy to under-advertise. We have endeavored to keep our advertising in several national magazines in good balance with our need for advertising at this time.

As the administrative head of the institution, I have endeavored, under God, and with the help of my staff, to steer all of the activities of the school on a course true to the principles set forth in our catalog. We have had an unusually high type of student on the average, and student morale has been high despite subtle and sustained satanic opposition from the outside.

As President of the College, I have endeavored, whether at the College or in the field through efficient organization, to keep in close touch with all phases of the College—the spiritual, the academic, the social, cultural, conferences, library, programs, athletics, counseling, discipline, stores, food-services, building and grounds, student procurement, purchasing, student employment, public relations, ad infinitum.

During the year I have preached many Chapel messages and taught a nominal load (using substitute teachers in my absence or making up sessions with irregularly scheduled classes). I have maintained office hours of from four to ten hours daily, usually six days a week when on campus making myself available for counseling with students, faculty and staff. I have maintained a daily administrative conference at which many details of the entire operation of the College were worked out. Since December 9th, I have pastored Berachah Baptist Church, preaching when in the city and using faculty, students, or visiting speakers to the spiritual welfare of the College and to guard against influences adverse to the philosophy of the College. Consequently we have regarded this ministry a direct and vital part of our service to the College.

During the year we have had many special events such as the following: Opening Evangelistic Meetings, Pan-Society programs, artists' programs, dramatic productions, choir tour, recitals, concerts, debates, class parties, Harvest Home Festival, faculty and each class entertained at the home of the President, conference on Evangelism and Missions, and many other student functions such as Halloween Party, Valentine Formal, Junior-Senior Banquet, etc. Over all of these affairs we have exercised some direction or guidance.

I have accepted all outside engagements with the twofold objective of serving in the various engagements to the glory of God on the local scene and of promoting the College to the glory of God. I have felt that every contact would accrue to the same twofold objective.

My engagements away from the College and Berachah Baptist Church during the last twelve months have included the following:

August 1964

    2—Indianapolis Baptist Temple, Indianapolis, Indiana
    3—Fundamental Baptist Pastors' Breakfast, Indianapolis
  17-22—Peoria Area C.B. Youth Camp, Muscatine, Iowa
    23—First Baptist Church, Hackensack, NJ

September 1964

    20—The Emmanuel Baptist Church, Pontiac, Michigan
  27-30—Citywide Evangelistic Campaign, Indianapolis, IN

October 1964

  1-18—Indianapolis Campaign Continued
  5- 6—Illinois State C.B.A., Chicago
  19-22—Central Regional, Chicago
  25-28—First Baptist Church, Albion, Michigan

November 1964

  12-15—Faith Baptist Church, LaCrosse, Wisconsin
  19-22—Calvary Baptist Church, Ottumwa, Iowa
  27-28—Minnesota Baptist Youth Rally, St. Paul
  29-30—Edgewood Baptist Church, Rock Island, Illinois

December 1964

  1- 6—Continue Rock Island
    16—Sword of the Lord Anniversary, First Baptist Church, Hammond, Indiana

January 1965

  11-12—W.C.B.M. Board Meetings, Chicago
    13—New Testament Baptist Council, Chicago
    31—Faith Baptist Church, Phoenix, Arizona

February 1965

  1- 7—Heart-to-Heart Chapel, Phoenix, Arizona
  10—Bob Jones University, Greenville, SC
  28—Fourth Baptist Church, Minneapolis

March 1965

  1- 3—Calvary Baptist Church, Portsmouth, Ohio
  7-10—Plymouth Baptist Church, Minneapolis
  14-17—Madison, Georgia
  22-23—First Baptist Church, Stewartville, Minnesota
  28-31—Canton Baptist Temple, Canton, Ohio

April 1965

  1- 4—Continue Canton, Ohio
  8-10—Faith Baptist Church, St. Paul
  14-19—Choir Tour
      14—Rockford, Illinois
      15—Constantine, Michigan
      16—Spring Lake, Michigan
      17—Port Huron, Michigan
      18—Detroit
          Springwells Avenue
          Joy Road
          Gratiot Avenue
      19—Chicago
      24—Fourth Baptist Sunday School Banquet, Curtis
          Hotel, Minneapolis
      25—First Baptist Church, Madelia, Minnesota
      27—Christian Bowlers' Banquet, Minneapolis

May 1965

  2- 5—First Baptist Church, Goodells, Michigan
  7- 8—Anaheim, California
      9—Central Seminary Baccalaureate
  13-16—First Baptist Church, Creve Coeur, Illinois
      18—Morristown, Minnesota
  28-29—New Testament Baptist Association, Denver
      30—A.M., Adams City Baptist Church
          P.M., South Sheridan Baptist Church, Denver, Col-
          orado

June 1965

      1—Bob Jones University, Greenville, SC

7- 9—Sword of the Lord Conference, Salem, Virginia
28-30—Sword of the Lord Conference, Jacksonville, Florida

July 1965

18-25—Scott Memorial Baptist Church, San Diego, California

In addition to these engagements, I have been active on the Boards of several associations and institutions.

June 30, 1965, brought to a close the Pillsbury fiscal year, 1964-65. The report of our auditor which I shall submit to you in a few minutes will reveal to you that we have had the most successful fiscal year by far in the eight-year history of the College.

This year, like the preceding ones, has been a very busy one and also a blessed one. We have seen 1200 decisions for Christ in our meetings, with scores of young people dedicating their lives for full-time Christian service.

I am grateful to you as a Board of Trustees for the faithful service and cooperation you have given me during the last year and the other seven years I have led the administration of our wonderful College. Be assured of my prayers for you and Dr. Cedarholm as you carry on this work which will remain dear to my heart. I will appreciate your prayers for me and my dear wife as we seek to serve the Lord Jesus Christ, the Holy Bible being our only rule of faith and practice.

CHAPTER XXVI

Move to Denver

Because there was no Christian high school in Owatonna and John was in high school and Penny in junior high school, we decided to move to Denver, where our friends, the Ed Nelsons, were beginning Silver State Baptist High School.

We loved living in Denver. We especially enjoyed being in South Sheridan Baptist Church and fellowship with Dr. and Mrs. Ed Nelson. Guyla Nelson and Marjorie and I had worked together at Bob Jones University when Marjorie was secretary to Dr. Bob Jones, Sr., and Guyla was secretary to Dr. Bob Jones, Jr., and I was Assistant to Dr. Bob Jones, Jr. Ed Nelson was a student in those days and was the president of the large preachers' class which I taught.

The long distance from Denver to the Midwest and the South and the West Coast made it expedient after John finished high school for us to move back to Alabama.

Return to Alabama

In February 1968, ten years after we left Decatur, we moved back there and purchased a home.

John attended Baptist Bible College in Denver and finished his college work at Covenant College on Lookout Mountain, Tennessee.

Penny graduated from Bob Jones University in 1973 and has taught in Christian high schools ever since—four years in the

United States, three in Canada, and for the last three years she has been on a missionary status with her local church and teaching in a Christian school in Belgium.

In November 1969 Dr. Lee Long resigned as General Director of Baptist World Mission, on whose board I served. The board asked me to take his place.

I answered that I planned to continue in full-time evangelistic work; but if they would agree to our moving the headquarters from Chicago to Decatur, Alabama, I would also serve the mission.

Baptist World Mission

In November 1969 the Baptist World Mission headquarters was moved to Decatur, and I became General Director. At that time we had six missionaries on three fields and eight under appointment with two additional fields approved.

I have carried on a full evangelistic program while also serving the mission. It would take volumes to tell of the multitudinous blessings that have come in "holding the ropes" for over one hundred missionaries on twenty-five fields. But it is a tremendous burden; and when my wife Marjorie, who served as office manager, was taken to Heaven in March, 1981, I had to have more help.

God had sent Mrs. Yvonne Braly to be our bookkeeper and Mrs. Jo Ann Huggins as secretary. These ladies are efficient and dedicated. But we needed someone to take Marjorie's place as office manager, and I needed an assistant. On May 1, 1981, God sent to us Dr. and Mrs. Fred Moritz. In 1984 I requested the board to make Dr. Moritz Executive Director. Dr. Moritz is a splendid evangelist and is eminently qualified to direct the mission. Although the board requested me to retain the title General Director, Dr. Moritz was promoted to Executive Director, and his lovely and efficient wife Judy is office manager.

CHAPTER XXVII

Another Dark Valley

When Marjorie died, I thought I would not marry again. I was seventy-one years of age; but I did not feel as I thought a septuagenarian was supposed to feel, and I was extremely lonely. I carried on my full program of evangelism and at Baptist World Mission. I had fellowship with the office staff, but Marjorie had been such an integral part of the mission work that I missed her at every turn. After her Homegoing March 14, 1981, life whether at home or away in a meeting was a lonely existence. Of course, I had the Lord, and He brought great comfort to me; and while we "sorrow not, even as others which have no hope," we do sorrow. For the first six months after Marjorie's death, I do not believe there was a single day in which I did not weep.

I would go to hold meetings and would go into a motel room. There was the telephone, but Marjorie would not be at the other end of the line.

After a while I began to realize that I needed a help meet for me. I made the following list of characteristics a woman must have if I should marry her:

1. She must be born again, and it must be apparent.
2. She must have the same philosophy of life that I hold. My philosophy is "for to me to live is Christ" (Phil. 1:21).
3. She must have the same objectives in life that I have.
4. She must have common sense.
5. She must have a sense of humor.

6. She must be dedicated to the Lord.
7. She must be dedicated to me in the Lord, realizing that "the buck stops here" (Eph. 5:22,23) when the husband is in subjection to the Lord (Eph. 5:25).
8. There must be between us that affinity, that mystique called "love."
9. She must be loyal.

In the summer of 1982 I flew down to South America with Bob Jones in the university plane. He asked me, "Monk, are you going to get married again?"

I answered, "I don't know, Bob. I get mighty lonely, but it would be hard to find a woman of the calibre of Harriette and Marjorie."

He said, "What about so and so?"

I answered, "I don't think so. She would not want to travel in evangelistic and mission work."

He said, "What about Mrs. Ed Whitley?"

I answered, "You might have something there."

He asked, "Would you like for me to contact her for you?"

I said, "Thanks, but I will do my own courting. I will be in North Carolina next fall, and I will check it out."

Light in the Valley

I had met Ed and Ruby Whitley once when I preached in their home church in Wilson, North Carolina. Brother Ed was a wonderful man and was a member of the Bob Jones University Board of Trustees on which board I have served since 1933. His wife, Ruby, used to come to the University with him, and I used to see her there although casually. Once she came with a delegation to a meeting I was holding in Rocky Mount, North Carolina. I knew she was a good active Christian, but I did not know her well.

In September of 1982 I went to Archer Weniger's funeral in California. After the funeral I rode with Bob Jones, Ian Paisley, and Rod Bell to the airport. We were escorted by police cars in front of us, beside us, and behind us in order to give Paisley safety while in America. We had supper, and Paisley had a flight for Ireland. Our flights were on Eastern and Delta, a few minutes apart. I exchanged my ticket on Eastern to ride on Delta with Bell and Jones. Bob asked me if I had been to North Carolina. I said, "No, but I will be in Durham and Greenville, North Carolina, in October."

He said, "Wilson is halfway between the two."

A Brief Courtship

I was in Durham for eight days; so I called Mrs. Whitley, whose husband had died four years previously, and asked if I might come over on Saturday and take her to lunch. She said, "That would be nice."

I liked her very much and figured that she would meet my requirements. I closed my meeting in Durham on Sunday night, left my car in Durham, and flew to Indiana to preach for the Mid-America Baptist Fellowship on Monday night. I flew back on Tuesday, got my car, and drove to Greenville, North Carolina, driving by Ruby's home in Wilson, but did not have time to stop.

Ruby's pastor at Tabernacle Baptist Church was Dr. Randy Carroll. The Carrolls were dear friends of mine. I had held meetings for them in three of his pastorates at Dixie, West Virginia, in the 1950's, in Sciotoville, Ohio, in the 1960's, and at Pratt, West Virginia, in 1963. Mrs. Carroll was one of Ruby's best friends. Ruby knew nothing of Baptist World Mission; but the Sunday I closed the meetings in Durham, Steven Krohn presented his work and his call to Puerto Rico at Tabernacle Baptist Church. He told the Carrolls that he wanted to go on to Greenville on Tuesday night where Dr. Monroe Parker was opening a revival meeting. Nancy Carroll got up a delegation, which included Ruby, to come to Greenville that night. I did not realize that Ruby was in the congregation until the service was dismissed and I met her in the aisle.

I made a luncheon date for the next day. We met at the

Colonial House in Farmville, and that day I knew she was the answer to my prayer. I went over to Wilson two more times that week; and since I was closing in Greenville Sunday morning, Dr. Carroll invited me to preach in Wilson Sunday night.

I proposed to Ruby and quoted Shakespeare's Petrucio, "My business asketh haste, and every day I cannot come to woo." But I kept the telephone lines hot.

Phil and Marie Shuler held a meeting in Wilson. Dr. Carroll told them that I had taken Ruby to dinner a couple of times. Phil wrote me that he was putting out a lot of propaganda about me to Ruby and sent me five dollars for a marriage license.

Yvonne Braly, bookkeeper at Baptist World Mission, invited Ruby to Decatur in November for a couple of days. I took an overnight flight from California, where I closed a meeting on Sunday night, and met Ruby's flight from Raleigh, North Carolina, in Atlanta, and we flew together on to Decatur. On Wednesday morning we were able to go to the airport together as she was going to North Carolina and I was flying to Colorado. I picked her up for breakfast at Hardee's. I almost swallowed my biscuit whole when, after nine weeks of pressure and prayer, she agreed to marry me.

My son, John, and my daughter, Penny, came home for Christmas. After Christmas dinner they both had to leave, and I lit out for Wilson, North Carolina. Ruby had Christmas dinner for me and her children and their families the evening of December 27.

Ruby has three daughters and a son, all of whom attended Bob Jones University. Her oldest daughter, Carol, is married to Larry Cox, who is a trumpeter par excellence, and they both teach in a Christian school in Pennsylvania. They have three children: Renee, Stephanie, and Larry, Jr.

Ruby's daughter Dianne is married to Grady Barnes, and they live in Wilson and have two sons, Brent and Trey.

Joe Edward Whitley, Jr., is in restaurant equipment business and lives near Wilson. His wife is named Beverly, and they now

My third wife, Ruby. We were married January 4, 1983.

have a baby a year old, Taylor Leigh, born two years after Ruby and I were married.

Ruby's youngest daughter is Beth. She and her husband, David Glover, are in the nursery business and have their large farm about ten miles from Wilson. They have three sons: David, Jr., Will, and Brian. Beth and my daughter Penny roomed in the same dormitory at Bob Jones University and were good friends.

We announced our engagement to her children at this dinner although they already suspected it. We told them it would probably be in February. However, December 28 is Ruby's birthday, and her daughter Beth had a dinner party for her that evening and invited a lot of Ruby's friends. They found out "confidentially." Wednesday night I preached for Dr. Carroll, and he announced it from the pulpit and asked us to go to the door in order that the people might greet us.

They filed by, many of the ladies kissing Ruby and weeping over her and congratulating me.

I said to Ruby, "That was like a wedding reception. We had just as well go ahead and get married."

She said, "I was just thinking about that."

After some persuasion she agreed to go ahead with our marriage the following Monday.

Neither of us wanted a big wedding. Ruby had lived in and near Wilson all of her life. She had many relatives of her own; and her former husband, who had died four years previously, had many relatives there. Her daughter Dianne with her husband and two boys had a short time before returned to Wilson from living in Kentucky and was living temporarily in Ruby's home with her. So Ruby could wait to sell her home. She asked me if I had just as soon be married at Bob Jones University. It pleased me greatly. We agreed to meet there at the Spartanburg-Greenville airport at 3:00 P.M. Monday.

I drove back to Decatur, Alabama, on Thursday and stopped overnight at a motel on the Greenville Bypass. I called Bob Jones and asked him if he could perform the ceremony at 5:00 P.M.

the following Monday. He said that would be fine. I had heard that South Carolina was no longer requiring a waiting period to get a marriage license.

Dr. and Mrs. Otis Holmes, dear friends of mine and also of Ruby's, having served several years as her pastor, met us at the airport and drove us to the courthouse, where we learned that they no longer required a blood test but required a waiting period of twenty-four hours for a license.

Mrs. Jones, Fannie Mae, had prepared a lovely "wedding dinner" for us and had invited a number of our friends and theirs. It turned out to be a "pre-wedding dinner." We were married in Dr. Jones' office at 5:00 P.M. Tuesday, January 14, 1983.

I Married a Wife

I had been booked to speak at a banquet in Brandon, Florida, on Tuesday night; so when I learned that we would have to wait until Tuesday for the wedding, I called the pastor, Dr. Vernon Nelms, and told him my plight. He said, "I will take the banquet engagement for you. What you are doing is more important. Come on and begin the meeting Wednesday night." When we began the meetings on Wednesday night, I said, "I was supposed to be here for a 'great supper' last night, but I married a wife and therefore I could not come."

After the wedding Dr. Otis Holmes drove us to the airport. Ruby had a dozen red roses that were sent to her by Mrs. Cathy Rice, a dear friend. The clerk at the Eastern Airlines gate said, "Have a seat here, please." In a few minutes he came to us and said, "Here is your seat assignment." It was in first class, although I had purchased second class tickets.

Dr. and Mrs. Nelms met us at the Tampa airport and drove us to the Holiday Inn on Fiftieth Street, where they had parked an extra car and where they had engaged the bridal suite for us. Dr. Nelms gave me the key to his new ninety-eight Oldsmobile and told us just to show up for evening services and, of course, the Sunday morning service.

After the Sunday evening service, the dear friends at Brandon Heights Baptist Church gave us a surprise reception, complete with a beautiful wedding cake. This was the first of several such receptions. When we returned to Decatur, friends there gave us a reception with another beautiful cake. We went to Wilson, and there they repeated the act at the Tabernacle Baptist Church. We went for a four-day meeting at Calvary Baptist Church, Lansdale, Pennsylvania. After the Tuesday night service, Pastor Bob Jordan had his staff to escort Ruby to the platform. They did so, singing a wedding song and bringing a lovely wedding cake to us. Next we went to Denver to hold meetings at South Sheridan Baptist Church. Dr. and Mrs. Ed Nelson and some ladies from the church had equipped an apartment at the Kipling Motel as a bridal suite and had laden the refrigerator and the shelves with goodies.

At this writing we have been married three years and seven months, and Ruby has been with me in all of my meetings—well over a hundred of them—and has proved to be a real blessing to the churches and a wonderful blessing to me.

CHAPTER XXVIII

A Wide Ministry

My ministry has extended over fifty-eight years. I have held over fifteen hundred evangelistic meetings, having preached in forty-six states and forty-three foreign countries. I have traveled in every state in the union and in fifty-five foreign countries. I have conducted eight tours to the Bible lands and have been there on several other occasions.

It was my privilege to preach in four of the six Fundamental Baptist Congresses of North America. I preached in Detroit in 1963 on "The Depravity of Man and the New Birth." I preached in the second Congress in Grand Rapids in 1966 on "Creation, Science, and Evolution," in the fifth Congress in 1974 in Detroit on "The Word of Faith," and in the sixth Congress in 1978 in Detroit on "Synthetic Religion."

It was my privilege to preach in two of the three World Fundamental Baptist Congresses. I preached at the Metropolitan Baptist Church (C. H. Spurgeon's church) in London on "Separated Unto the Gospel of God," and in Jerusalem on "Out of the Ivory Palaces." It was my privilege to preach in three of the four World Congresses of Fundamentalists. I preached in Manila in 1980 on "What Is the Gospel?" At the World Congress at Bob Jones University in 1983 I preached on "The Inspiration of the Bible" and at the Congress in 1986 on "Missions, Its Tedium."

I am appending the sermon I preached in the sixth Fundamental Baptist Congress of North America on the subject of "Synthetic Religion."

In 1972 I spent the month of September as the guest of Dr. Ian Paisley in Northern Ireland. I conducted a two-week campaign in the Martyrs' Memorial Free Presbyterian Church and had souls to come to Christ in every service. Then I went with Dr. Paisley on one-night stands all over Northern Ireland, where we both preached. On the last Sunday I was in Ireland, I preached for Dr. Paisley's father, who was the long-time pastor of the First Baptist Church of Balamena.

My wife took excerpts from my letters while I was in Northern Ireland. They are as follows:

> Dr. Paisley and his bodyguard and one of the pastors met me at the airport. There was a riot here yesterday afternoon; and as we drove through town, about four blocks of the street were filled with broken bottles, rocks, etc. The pastor who brought me to the hotel drove me by to show me the site of a $30,000,000 building they destroyed completely with their bombings.

> I am to be here in Belfast fifteen days in Dr. Paisley's church, and then Dr. Paisley and I are going to hold one-night meetings in various cities of Northern Ireland the third week with both of us preaching.

> I haven't heard any bombs today although I heard two yesterday morning and one last night. One of them was a bakery. It was completely destroyed. We had a good beginning here, had a tremendous crowd last night. The people are really praying for a revival. Paisley is a remarkable man. He is tremendous. He prays, sings, and speaks with all that in him is.

> We had a 7:00 o'clock prayer meeting this morning and will each morning as well as one at seven each night. There were about 40 there this morning, and how they prayed! These people are conscious of impending death. I see it more here in the hotel than I see it in the people at the church. There, although it is ameliorated by faith, you can tell in their prayers and their conversation that they are conscious that death stalks the streets.

> A lady living here at the hotel told me that her house was destroyed by bombs and that is why she is here. Genesis 6:11 says, "The earth also was corrupt before God, and the earth was filled

Looking at papers I brought from Northern Ireland.

with violence." That was said of Noah's day but could certainly be applied to our time.

Last night a bomb was thrown into a home here in Belfast, and a woman visiting there was killed and two others badly injured. The home was completely demolished. Another bomb was placed in a car, and a young man passing by in another car as the bomb went off was killed. Hundreds of windows were broken. Two men were found shot on the street. A pub was blown up here in Belfast; and up at Balamena there were two explosions, wrecking two places of business and killing two people. They were in Dr. Paisley's constituency. This is going on night and day. Yet we are having wonderful crowds and good meetings. The people are expecting a sweeping revival. I pray that it will come.

It seems that the British soldiers who are here to protect the people against the IRA have got pretty highhanded; and although the Ulsterites want British citizenship and, in fact, want even closer union with Britain, they resent some of the actions of the army. It is complicated, and I will have to wait until I get home to explain it. Paisley is a moderating force. If it were not for him, there would have been civil war already. As it is, there is uncivil war going on.

No trouble today except that a wine and beer shop was blown up, and two men were shot by gunmen passing in a red minicar. All stores, banks, hotels, and other places here have armed guards, and you are checked as you enter. The doors in this hotel are kept locked; and you have to ring a bell, and a guard comes to let you in.

I went downtown to get my ticket changed at the BEA office and had to walk a couple of blocks through barbed wire barricades manned by the English army. It was in the area of downtown closest to the Catholic district. The IRA has threatened to blow up a big hospital if they don't remove soldiers from its premises.

Last night was a night of violence as usual. It is intensifying. There were eight bombings yesterday and last night and three murders. The nearest bomb to my hotel was three blocks away. One hotel similar to this one was blown to bits. A bomb was in a car (an eight-pound bomb), and a passerby saw it smoking and warned the people; so they nearly all got out of the hotel before the explosion. But an old folks' home across the street was wrecked; a man driving by was killed, and in all forty-nine others were injured. Twice this week people have been killed driving by when car bombs have exploded. I went to the Paisleys after the service last night and was there until midnight. It sounded like a war. Bombs kept going off.

We are having surprisingly large crowds and good services, but a lot of people are afraid to go out. But one never knows when a bomb will be thrown in his house; so they had as well come to church. People have been warned not to pick up matches, fountain pens, cigarette lighters, or match boxes; they may be booby traps. One has to be careful in a public phone booth. Yesterday a bomb was placed in a locker at a golf course and blew down the pro house. But in all this I feel perfectly safe. I am in Psalm 91 and Psalm 23:4.

Things are getting worse here according to reports. More violence last night! That sounds trite. Have got to go back behind the barbed-wire barriers today to pick up my ticket which I left at the BEA office on Monday for a change in schedule.

Dr. Paisley took me to the Europa Hotel for supper last night. They really have it barricaded. There have been six attempts to blow it up. Extensive damage was done, but it has been repaired. He thought I would be safer in this small hotel.

CHAPTER XXIX

What Prayer Can Do

In my long life I have learned that not everybody who says that he loves everybody does so. Liberals claim that they love more than fundamentalists, but it seems that their motto is, "I hate you because you don't love me."

Moses loved his people so much that he prayed if God would not forgive their sin, "blot me out of the book which thou hast written" (Exod. 32:32). Yet when Moses saw that the people were worshiping the golden calf and that they "were naked; (for Aaron had made them naked unto their shame among their enemies" (Exod. 32:25), he had about three thousand of them slain.

Moses loved his people, but he loved justice and truth and the glory of God more.

I have learned that there is a sickly sentimentalism some people call love which is not love but in its final analysis is only selfishness.

The kindest, most thoughtful, and loving people I have ever known have been fundamentalists. I have learned as a whole they are less hypocritical. So-called liberals are subtle. A unitarian in a trinitarian pulpit is a hypocrite.

In many years as an evangelist, I have learned that prayer will bring revival. I wrote the following article in 1952 for Clifford Lewis' magazine, *Living Faith*:

PRAYER WILL BRING REVIVAL

In January I was in Roslyn, Pennsylvania, in the Philadelphia area. I was impressed with the fact that people came to Christ at every opportunity; and on several occasions, when I had addressed my messages to Christians, I felt constrained to give the invitation, and people were saved. One day during this campaign, I spoke to the staff of the *Sunday School Times* and there met two elderly ladies. One was an employee of the *Times*; and the other, a worker of the Scripture Gift Mission. They told me that they had covenanted together to pray each day for my ministry; and among other things, they were asking God to give me souls every time I preached.

In my next campaign in Zion, Illinois, I had a similar experience. This time it was a dear old man eighty-eight years of age who got out of bed at four o'clock every morning to pray for me, and I have his word that he will continue the practice until God takes him home.

Many others were praying faithfully during the Zion meeting. There we experienced a genuine revival among the Christian people, with many sinners coming to Christ. The revival reached into the local high school in a very special way. Among those converted were the captain and the co-captain of the football team and the captain of the wrestling team. Naturally this brought tremendous response from the high school. The young people went to the principal and asked if he would have the evangelistic party for a chapel service.

His policies would not allow him to do this, but these young converts were so enthusiastic that on their own initiative they drew up a petition requesting the administration to make an exception in this case and have us for a chapel service. The petition was signed by all the students, including Roman Catholics, Jews, Russellites, Seventh-Day Adventists, etc. Such was the revival spirit that in spite of sub-zero weather, we saw a blessed revival in Zion.

We were next in Terre Haute, Indiana. There was not a single service without conversions. Cottage prayer meetings were held each day, and large numbers of people were imploring God in earnest prayer for each service held. He poured out abundant blessings upon the meeting; many backsliders were reclaimed, and many souls were saved.

During the meeting I received a telegram from a friend, a businessman in West Chester, Pennsylvania, saying that he was setting aside one hour a day to pray for me. Unworthy though I am, I thank God for the thousands of people who pray daily for God's blessings upon my ministry. I dare say that every evangelist whom God is using in an unusual way today could tell a similar story.

In Roslyn, Pennsylvania, Pastor George Slavin prepared some booklets emphasizing the importance of prayer and containing a space for prayer lists. On the flyleaf were these lines: "Little prayer, little power; more prayer, more power; much prayer, much power." How faithfully God answers prayer and yet how faithless most Christian people are in this vital ministry! When the Israelites were in trouble and asked Samuel to pray for them, he answered, "God forbid that I should sin against the Lord in ceasing to pray for you."

I am writing these lines from Dania, Florida, where we are engaged in a campaign in a large tent. The meetings are sponsored by the Dania Heights Baptist Church. It is the height of the tourist season in this great American Playground, and excitement runs high. People do not have much time for God. It seems that they are either here to play or they are bent on making all the money possible while the season is on and while the "making" is good.

In spite of this, we are beginning to see revival, and it is the result of prayer. Never in my life have I been more burdened for an individual than I have for a young man here. I have prayed earnestly for his conversion for the past four days. He accepted the challenge of a friend who told him that he could not hear me preach five times without being converted. Last night was his third service and, praise God, he was gloriously saved. With him was his Roman Catholic sweetheart, and she, too, accepted Christ and with him joined this Baptist church. Others were saved last night for whom many have been praying. Prayer is the thing that will bring revival!

The prayer Jesus prayed when He was on the cross, "Father, forgive them; for they know not what they do," was full of significance. It was a prayer to be heard by God the Father, but it was also loaded with lessons for you and me. In praying this prayer, Jesus taught us the importance of prayer. He was nailed to a cross of wood, and His mighty passion held Him there. He could no longer go about on errands of mercy, but He could pray, and that He did.

He prayed for those who knew not what they were doing,

and it was to these who through ignorance "crucified the Lord of glory" that Peter preached fifty days later. Three thousand of them were converted. They were not converted because of the eloquence of Peter although he spoke with boldness as the Holy Spirit gave him utterance. They were not converted just because it was the Day of Pentecost and the Holy Spirit was now in the bodies of men and the prophecy of Joel had to be fulfilled. This demonstration could have been enacted among people who had not participated in the mockery of Calvary's cross. But many of those very people were saved in answer to the prayer of Jesus. In this prayer He taught us to regard no one beyond the reach of the power of prayer, not even religious bigots steeped in prejudice and pride or cruel sadists who could jeer and laugh at a dying Christ. Jesus prayed. He prayed until Heaven heard, and the greatest revival in the history of the world broke out among those who through ignorance "crucified the Lord of glory." Oh, let us pray!

I am often asked when I plan to retire. I don't plan to retire. Retirement is fine for some people who have worked hard and in their old age need to take it easy or for people who are ill. Of course, I may get infirm and find it necessary to stop one day. In the meantime, however, I shall press on.

I heard Munhall preach when he was ninety-two. He was vigorous and alert and had great power.

I heard A. C. Gaebelein when he was way up in his eighties, and he was keen-minded and forceful.

I heard Robert G. Lee when he was ninety. He quoted the second chapter of Titus and preached like a young man.

Well, writing an autobiography is a clumsy experience. I did not know what to call the book. I named it THROUGH SUNSHINE AND SHADOWS: *My First Seventy-Seven Years.* To close an autobiography is also rather frustrating; so I shall just say, "To Be Continued."

Synthetic Religion

Monroe Parker, Ph.D., D.D.

"Ye shall keep my statutes. Thou shalt not let thy cattle gender with a diverse kind: thou shalt not sow thy field with mingled seed: neither shall a garment mingled of linen and woollen come upon thee" —Lev. 19:19.

A generation ago a favorite question of the modernists was, "What is a modernist, anyway?" Today the new evangelicals are asking, "What is a new evangelical?" Of course, there are millions of Christian people who do not know what a new evangelical is. For the benefit of such people, as well as for those new evangelicals who think fundamentalists are so naive as to believe that they do not know what a new evangelical is, these lines are written.

A new evangelical is not necessarily a modernist, although many of those who are known as new evangelicals are modernists.

A new evangelical is not necessarily neo-orthodox, although many of those who are known as new evangelicals are neo-orthodox.

A new evangelical is not necessarily an evangelical, although many new evangelicals are evangelical.

Certain astute new evangelicals have begun asking the question, "What is a new evangelical?" because they recognize that new evangelicalism, if given theological classification, would fall into the Department of Practical Theology. It does not lay stress on doctrinal content. If new evangelicalism is not defined in the terms of any particular doctrinal position, it would seem rather bigoted to oppose it. On the other hand, practical theology is theology, a science as well as an art, and, of course, has doctrinal ramifications.

Unscriptural Alliance

New evangelicalism, strictly speaking, was sired by an irresponsible effort on the part of some evangelicals to lure men to an acceptance of Christ as Saviour through unscriptural alliances, and in some cases through open appeal to the lust of the flesh, the lust of the eye, and the pride of life.

Some sincere people have been caught in the vortex of the movement, but let us not forget that one can be sincere and still be wrong. Conscience is not a safe guide unless the light of truth shines upon it. A man's conscience is governed by what he believes.

New evangelicalism was born of the confusion which followed the confessed failure of modernism in the crises of World War II. At that time hundreds of leading modernists confessed that they had gone too far from the pole of truth, the supernatural revelation of God in the Holy Bible and in Jesus Christ, the Son of God, and they became willing to accept neo-orthodoxy; and many evangelicals thought they had been converted.

With an orthodox profession, but still holding their old philosophy of naturalism, the modernists lacked the conviction to proclaim their new message, refill their churches, and replenish their coffers. Many gifted liberals were able to adapt, but few could sound a positive note; they had spoken too long in the accents of surmise and speculation.

Evangelicals Enlisted

Their recourse was to enlist evangelicals. This they could not do directly. It would require great skill and "statesmanship" and compromise with evangelicals beyond the point many liberals were willing to go. It could be accomplished only at the summit where key leaders could court key leaders.

Thus began a great compromise. I heard the great liberal preacher, Dr. Paul Shearer, declare in 1946 that the modernists needed to retrace their footsteps back toward the old orthodox position of their fathers, but that they should not go all the way back. He said the modernists should form a synthesis with the evangelicals. Four years later I heard Dr. Sidlow Baxter, the great British evangelical, speak to the faculties of the Bible Institute of Los Angeles and Fuller Theological Seminary. It was a "closed door meeting" in the Church of the Open Door. He said that he had found a schism in the church of America which was not so marked in the Church of England. He said that while he stood doctrinally with the conservatives, those on the other side of the gap were disillusioned men, and so they were. I could say, "Amen," to that. I could not agree with his conclusion, however. He said that Bible-believing Christians ought to bridge the gap in fellowship. But light cannot have "fellowship with darkness," and "he that believeth" has "no part with an infidel." "Thou shalt not sow thy field with mingled seed."

In September 1950 Dr. John MacKay, one of the founders of the World Council of Churches and the most outstanding leader of the ecumenical movement, speaking at the opening of the academic year at Princeton Theological Seminary, of which he was then president, said: "This past summer I passed through Portland, Oregon, at a time when the evangelist Billy Graham was being listened to by crowds of over one hundred thousand. I learned that churches in the great Oregon city were getting behind that simple, non-college-trained man, an intimate friend of our own Charles Templeton. The churches cannot ignore the phenomenon which this young man presents. And then there is the Youth for Christ movement, the Inter-Varsity movement, the Pentecostals—all of whom are doing an amazing work in many parts of the world. These groups are often frowned on as

Christianity's 'lunatic fringe' because of certain objectionable features which they manifest. Yet according to the clear evidence of spiritual results, they are doing a great work in which God is present. As to the fruits that may be garnered from these movements into the storehouse of the Christian church, that will depend upon the sympathy, the good judgment, and the statesmanship of the Christian churchmen. Among the things which I have learned in my lifetime, both by experience and observation, is this: Never to be afraid of a young fanatic or of what appears to be a fanatical movement, if Jesus Christ is the supreme object of devotion. . . . The young fanatic, if wisely dealt with, can be toned down and mellowed."

Remember, that statement was made in 1950 at Princeton. In 1957 Dr. MacKay was among the sponsors of Billy Graham's New York campaign.

Billy Graham

I am often asked if I agree with Dr. Graham in his program. It is difficult for me to answer because I love Billy Graham personally. I have known him well since he was seventeen years of age and consider him a personal friend. He has been so signally blessed of God and has won so many people to Christ that it is difficult for me to say that I do not agree with the policies he has followed since 1957. However, I have told him personally that he is neutralizing his good.

A man criticized me and said that I ought not to criticize Billy Graham because he had won more souls to Christ than I. I believe I have won more souls to Christ than the man who criticized me, but that does not make me immune to criticism. The Apostle Peter had 3,000 converts in a single service, but that did not place him above the just rebuke and criticism of Paul at Antioch.

In the sacred task of preaching the Word of God, collaboration with those who do not believe the cardinal doctrines of the Christian Faith is wrong, no matter who does it.

I rode on Billy Graham's "bandwagon" from the time of his 1949 Los Angeles Campaign until I read the message and heard the tape of the message he preached at Union Theological Seminary in 1955, in which he threw bricks at the fundamentalists and roses at the modernists.

When this message was published by Dr. Carl McIntyre in *The Christian Beacon,* Billy Graham was in his great Scotland campaign. A friend of Dr. Graham's paid Dr. John Rice's way to Scotland to be a guest of Dr. Graham. Dr. Rice helped Billy pull his chestnuts out of the fire, so to speak. He felt that Billy had certainly been unwise in making the statements he made at Union Seminary but felt that he was young and that he would certainly listen to the advice of his conservative friends.

Dr. Rice wrote a featured article in THE SWORD OF THE LORD, reporting the Scotland campaign and giving Billy Graham the benefit of the doubt as to his courting or favoring liberals for their support. Later when Billy went to New York under the sponsorship of the modernistic Protestant Council of Churches and announced at Buffalo to the National Association of Evangelicals that he would accept the sponsorship of modernists, Dr. Rice was forced to the conclusion that Billy had taken the wrong direction.

In April 1958 I said the following to Dr. Graham: "Billy, I give you the benefit of any doubts as to motives. I believe you are trying to take advantage of the friendly gestures of liberals toward conservatives. You are using the liberals in order to get a chance to preach the Gospel to thousands of people in modernistic churches. But these liberals are using you, and though you are doing some good, it is being neutralized. You are not isolated. Few men have more influence than you. Hundreds of other evangelists and pastors feel that they must follow your example and your methods. I urge you to return to your former policy of being sponsored by evangelicals only."

Some weeks later I signed my name to a friendly letter of greeting containing the same appeal which was written by an outstanding Baptist pastor from the East and was also signed by scores of other Christian leaders during the annual meetings of Conservative Baptists at Denver, Colorado. It grieves many of us who know and love him that he did not follow this advice.

I am not writing in a bigoted spirit. I realize that if I had my just deserts, I would be in Hell. But I am saved by the grace of God. I love this glorious Gospel and love Christ and love the souls of men. That is why I am against anything that would weaken the Christian testimony and pervert the church of Christ. New evangelicalism will do just that.

System Not Acceptable

I heard Dr. Vernon Grounds say at the Colorado State meetings of Conservative Baptists in May 1959 that anything that is good in new evangelicalism is of God. If this is true, does it follow that anything that is good in Christian Science, or Communism, or Mormonism, or Seventh-Day Adventism is of God? Whether this is so, it does not follow that the entire system is of God. It is just as logical to conclude that anything that is bad in new evangelicalism is of the world, the flesh, or the Devil.

In its beginning new evangelicalism was not characterized by doctrinal content but by method. This method is that of joining with enemies of the true Gospel in an effort to promote the Gospel while they promote a contrary message. Every child of God ought to repudiate new evangelicalism.

God's Answer to New Evangelicalism

John, the apostle of love, wrote: "If there come any unto you, and bring not this doctrine, receive him not into your house, neither bid him God speed: For he that biddeth him God speed is partaker of his evil deeds" (II John 10, 11). What is God's answer to new evangelicalism? God's answer to new evangelicalism is also found in II Corinthians 6:14, 16-18: "Be ye not unequally yoked together with unbelievers: for what fellowship hath righteousness with unrighteousness? and what communion hath light with darkness?... And what agreement hath the temple of God with idols? for ye are the temple of the living God; as God hath said, I will dwell in them, and walk in them; and I will be their God, and they shall be my people. Wherefore come out from among them, and be ye separate, saith the Lord, and touch not the unclean thing: and I will receive you, And will be a Father unto you, and ye shall be my sons and daughters, saith the Lord Almighty."

Having lain down with the dogs of liberalism, the new evangelicals have got up with doctrinal fleas on themselves.

They decided to treat evolution as a moot question, and many of them have embraced theistic evolution.

They decided not to be "other worldly"; and the result, the "Doctrine of Balaam" or worldliness.

They decided to follow a philosophy of pragmatism, and the result is an exalting of feeling and experience above "thus saith the Lord." Hence, so-called revelations, and charismatic manifestations.

They decided to add to the Gospel the social gospel; hence, a synthetic religion.

Day of Compromise

The new evangelicals have failed to heed the warning of Jesus to "Beware of wolves in sheep's clothing." It seems that we have reached a day of compromise on every hand. Even earnest, evangelical Christians censure the servants of God who cry out against false prophets. But these servants of God are in a glorious tradition.

Old Testament Prophets Denounced False Religious Leaders

Isaiah cried out against the priest and prophet who "err in vision" and "stumble in judgment" (Isa. 28:7). Jeremiah said, "For both prophet and priest are profane; yea, in my house have I found their wickedness, saith the Lord" (Jer. 24:11). Ezekiel wrote, "Thus saith the Lord God; Woe unto the foolish prophets that follow their own spirit, and have seen nothing! O, Israel, thy prophets are like the foxes in the deserts" (Ezek. 13:3, 4). Micah said, "They build up Zion with blood, and Jerusalem with iniquity. The heads thereof judge for reward, and the priests thereof teach for hire, and the prophets thereof divine for money: yet will they lean upon the Lord, and say, Is not the Lord among us?" (Mic. 3:10, 11).

Jesus and Apostles Denounced False Religious Leaders

Jesus Christ, the Lord of Glory, said, "Beware of false prophets." The Apostle Peter, speaking of the scoffers who sneer at the promise of the coming of Christ and wrest the Scripture unto their own destruction, said, "Beware lest ye also, being led away with the error of the wicked, fall from your own steadfastness" (II Pet. 3:17). Paul, the missionary, evangelist, apostle, and builder of churches, the bondslave of Jesus Christ, wrote to Timothy, "But after their own lusts shall they heap to themselves teachers having itching ears; and they shall turn away their ears from the truth, and shall be turned unto fables. But watch thou in all things, endure afflictions, do the work of an evangelist, make full proof of thy ministry. For I am now ready to be offered, and the time of my departure is at hand. I have fought a good fight, I have finished my course, I have kept the faith" (II Tim. 4:3-7). To the church at Rome he wrote, "Now I beseech you, brethren, mark them which cause divisions and offenses contrary to the doctrine which ye have learned; and avoid them. For they that are such serve not our Lord Jesus Christ, but their own belly; and by good words and fair speeches deceive the hearts of the simple" (Rom. 16:17, 18). John the Beloved, who wrote his Gospel that we "might believe that Jesus is the Christ, the Son of God" (John 10:31), wrote in his second epistle, "If there come any unto you, and bring not this doctrine, receive him not into your house, neither bid him God speed" (II John 10). Jude wrote, "For there are certain men crept in

unawares, who were before of old ordained to this condemna-
tion, ungodly men, turning the grace of our God into
lasciviousness, and denying the only Lord God, and our Lord
Jesus Christ" (Jude 4). He says that they are "raging waves of
the sea, foaming out their own shame; wandering stars, to whom
is reserved the blackness of darkness for ever" (Jude 13).

If the Blind Lead

Thousands of young theological students are gullibly following these "false prophets in sheep's clothing" who "within are
ravening wolves." Impressed by the high-sounding theological
terminology, the vast store of encyclopedic knowledge, and the
pious talk of false teachers, thousands of them are going out
themselves in "sheep's clothing" to preach the new modernism.
"If the blind lead the blind, both shall fall into the ditch" (Mat.
15:14). Tragedy of tragedies! The new modernism is as false as
the old! It is essentially the same though covered in a new robe
and a thousand times more subtle.

Need Today for Exposing False Teaching

There was never a day when fundamentalists needed more to
emphasize the verbal inspiration of the Bible and the deity of
the Lord Jesus Christ than today. They need also to understand
the issues and the design of these new modernists. Many of our
true evangelical leaders must surely be uninformed as to the
ultimate aim of some of the ecclesiastical leaders. It is
Nicolaitanism—the conquering of the laity. No one who believes
in a congregational form of church government and in the right
of the individual to interpret the Word of God for himself under
the illumination of the Holy Spirit can follow these false
teachers. Let us look under the "sheep's clothing" and there we
see the pointed ears, the leering eyes, the dilated nostrils, the
dripping tongues, and the bared fangs of "ravening wolves."

Purpose of Liberal Leaders

What is the design of these men? Back of this movement is a plan for the formation of one World Church. As has already been said, the modern church had lost its voice of authority because it had left the authority of the Scriptures. The Catholics believe in an authoritative church with an infallible Pope at the head of it. Although they accept the Bible as infallible, they hold it is so only as it is interpreted by the church. Orthodox Protestantism has held to the infallibility of the Bible by which the church is judged. The new modernism is attempting to recover authority for the purpose of building ecclesiastical walls, but is unwilling to yield to the inerrant and infallible authority of full, verbal inspiration. Consequently, just as the British crown is a symbol of British authority with the authority vested in Parliament, so the new modernism is trying to make the Bible a symbol of authority with the authority actually vested in the church.

Substitute for Inspiration Offered

Dr. John Newton Thomas, Professor of Systematic Theology at Union Theological Seminary, Richmond, Virginia, wrote in an article in the July 1946 issue of *Theology Today,* page 171: "Is not the key to the situation the frank acknowledgement of the Church's authority as determiner of the Canon? This is at once the valid substitute for the doctrine of verbal inspiration and the guarantee of an authoritative Scripture as against rationalizing and mystical influences."

There you have it, my friends. These liberals are determined to form through their councils a church arrogating to itself the authority to change the Bible to suit their doctrine. Professor Thomas goes on to say: "If the current re-emphasis upon the Church can secure recognition of her true and legitimate role in relation to the Canon, we shall emerge from the present confusion with a clearer grasp of the authority both of the Church and of the Bible" (Ibid., p. 171). There is no wonder that the National Council of Churches has no compunction against shading the Word of God as in the Revised Standard Version to favor its liberal theology. They have usurped for themselves the authority to speak for God instead of simply recognizing that God has spoken.

The same issue of *Theology Today* (July 1946) in which Professor Thomas' article is found carries an article by Floyd V. Filson, Professor of New Testament Literature and History, McCormick Theological Seminary, on "The Revised Standard New Testament" (page 221) in which he says, "The Bible is the Church's book." The professor is wrong. It is God's Book. He says further, "Its writers were members and servants of the Church, and their writings have been preserved, translated, and used in its worship, preaching, and teaching. The real test, therefore, which this version must pass is whether it will prove adequate to the needs of the Church." The real test is whether it is true to the original text written by "holy men of old" as they were "moved by the Holy Ghost."

Need to Recognize Authority of Word

The greatest need in the church today is not a "substitute for the doctrine of verbal inspiration" but a realization that here we have the very inspired Word of the Living God whether correctly or incorrectly interpreted. It is "more to be desired than gold, yea, than much fine gold; sweeter also than honey and the honeycomb" (Ps. 19:10). Let us hide it in our hearts, live it in our daily walk, preach it to the world, teach it to our children, and beware lest "false prophets in sheep's clothing" steal it away!

Precious promise God hath given to the weary passerby,
On the way from earth to Heaven, "I will guide thee with Mine eye."

In these days when the world is in such turmoil and millions of voices are clamoring to be heard, may God help us to speak out with the Word of divine authority, the Bible. "All scripture is given by inspiration of God, and is profitable for reproof. . . ." Therefore, "Reprove"! (II Tim. 4:2). It is profitable "for instruction in righteousness" (II Tim. 3:16). Therefore, "Exhort with all longsuffering and doctrine" (II Tim. 4:2).

This blessed Book is the daily bread which God has provided for His hungry children. Feast upon it, my fainting friend. It is the water of life springing from the fountain of divine inspiration. Quaff it, O thirsty soul! It is the staff which God has given to the weary pilgrim. Lean upon it! It is the Sword of truth from Heaven's arsenal. Brandish it, Christian soldier! You are in the "conflict of the ages," but look out for camouflage!

> Faith of our fathers! living still
> In spite of dungeon, fire, and sword;
> O how our hearts beat high with joy
> Whene'er we hear that glorious word!
> Faith of our fathers! holy faith!
> We will be true to thee till death!

The World's Most Popular Game

Evangelistic Sermon by
Dr. Monroe Parker

"I have sinned: return, my son David: for I will no more do thee harm, because my soul was precious in thine eyes this day: behold, I have played the fool, and have erred exceedingly." —
I Sam. 26:21.

The most popular game in the world is not necessarily played on the gridiron, the basketball court, the baseball field, the ice rink, or in the gymnasium. It may be played anywhere. It is a universal game and has been played in all ages.

Saul Played the Popular Game

Saul, the son of Kish, played this game three thousand years ago when he became inflated with pride, fell into sin, realized his folly and became jealous of David, who now held the esteem of his people, which he had so shamefully lost. David was fleeing from the jealous king and for the second time spared the king's life when he could easily have taken it. The first time, Saul had stopped to rest in the mouth of a cave in the wilderness of En-gedi, and David, who was concealed in the cave, cut the skirt from Saul's robe. Saul knew nothing of it until he had left the cave and David came out and called to him and showed him the skirt from his robe. Saul wept and confessed that he was wrong and that God's favor was with David. He conceded that

David would become king and returned to his home.

David Spares Saul Again

Now Saul's jealousy had overcome him again and he was seeking David's life. He followed David into the wilderness of Ziph. Here he stopped for the night while Saul slept in a trench with Abner and his soldiers slept all around him. David stole into Saul's camp and took Saul's spear and a cruse of water that was by his side. He then went over on the hill across the valley and cried out, rebuking Abner and saying, "As the Lord liveth, ye are worthy to die, because ye have not kept your master, the Lord's anointed" (I Sam. 26:16).

When Saul realized that David had stood above him as he slept with spear in hand but that he had spared his life the second time, he said, "I have sinned: return, my son David: for I will no more do thee harm, because my soul was precious in thine eyes this day: behold, I have played the fool, and have erred exceedingly" (I Sam. 26:21).

"I have sinned. . . I have played the fool." That heart-rending cry has been ringing down the ages and every man, woman, boy, and girl who ever drew a breath of air, except our blessed Lord Jesus Christ, has at some time played the game of sin and thereby played the fool.

Playing the Fool Is Popular Play

First, the one who sins plays the fool. It is foolish to sin, because sin is against God, against others, and against self.

Sin Is Against God

When David confessed his great sin to God he said, "Against thee, thee only, have I sinned, and done this evil in thy sight" (Ps. 51:4). Later in his prayer he declared that if he were restored to fellowship and blessing, he would teach transgressors the way of the Lord and sinners would be converted to Him. Others were affected not only by David's act of sin, but also by David's estrangement from God.

Sin has an effect upon the one who is playing the game. In David's case his joy was gone, his power was gone, and that awful sense of guilt overwhelmed his soul.

Sin Grieves God

To commit sin is foolish because it grieves God and robs Him of His glory. "Because that, when they knew God, they glorified him not as God, neither were thankful; but became vain in their imaginations, and their foolish heart was darkened. Professing themselves to be wise, they became fools, And changed the glory of the uncorruptible God into an image made like to corruptible man, and to birds, and fourfooted beasts, and creeping things" (Rom. 1:21-23).

The sins of Saul brought grief to the Lord and to Samuel, His prophet. After Saul's disobedience in sparing Agag, the king of the Amalekites, we read, "And Samuel came no more to see Saul until the day of his death: nevertheless Samuel mourned for Saul: and the Lord repented that he had made Saul king over Israel" (I Sam. 15:35).

Sinner, you have no idea how your sins grieve the heart of God. Every sin of your life was upon Jesus Christ when He hanged on the cross of Calvary. And He felt the weight of it in His soul which had infinite capacity to suffer. Every oath, every dirty word, every lie, every hateful, unkind word spoken against the Holy Trinity, or the Holy Bible, whether in an effort to destroy the true faith or to build up a false religion, dishonors Christ and grieves the great heart of God. Every effort to enthrone man in God's place is an effort to dethrone God.

Every act of aggression toward others or every wrong attitude toward others—theft, adultery, murder, lust, hate, false witness, or covetousness—is an act against God or a wrong attitude toward God. It is foolish to sin, because it is against God, and man is a fool to oppose the Almighty.

"Behold, I have sinned. . . I have played the fool," confessed the haughty king.

Sin Is Against Others

I talked with an old drunkard in the Evansville Rescue Mission in Evansville, Indiana, one night. He kept saying that his sins were not hurting anyone but himself. During the service he fell under conviction for his sins and responded to the invitation. Then he began to talk about how he had wronged his wife and children. He had left them ragged, cold, and hungry without a source of livelihood. You cannot sin without affecting others. The sins of Saul affected all of Israel. Saul's son, Jonathan, was not to reign in Saul's stead, because of the sins of Saul. It is foolish to sin, because it is against one's fellows, and one is a fool to wrong the society of which he is a part, whether it be the home, the municipality, the state, or society in general.

Sin Is Against Self

It is foolish to sin, because it is against one's self, and one is a fool to injure himself. There is a law of spiritual harvest. "Whatsoever a man soweth, that shall he also reap. For he that soweth to his flesh shall of the flesh reap corruption" (Gal. 6:7,8).

When Saul was anointed king over Israel, he was very humble. When lots were taken at Mizpeh to determine who should be king and the lot fell to the family of Kish and then to Saul, they found Saul hidden among the stuff (I Sam. 10:22). But after Saul had reigned two years he had become proud and self-willed. When he thought Samuel was late in coming to Gilgal where they were to meet, he arrogantly entered into the sanctuary, usurping the authority of a priest, and offered sacrifice.

Saul's Dynasty Rejected

When Saul told Samuel what he had done, Samuel said, "Thou hast done foolishly: thou hast not kept the commandment of the Lord thy God, which he commanded thee: for now would the Lord have established thy kingdom upon Israel for ever. But now thy kingdom shall not continue" (I Sam. 13:13, 14).

Saul's sin affected the Lord; it affected Saul's family and his kingdom, and it affected himself. Saul played the fool when he intruded into the office of the priest, because "the way of a fool is right in his own eyes" (Prov. 12:15); he played the fool, because "a fool's wrath is presently known" (Prov. 12:16) and "anger resteth in the bosom of fools" (Eccles. 7:9), in his failure to give obedience to God's command to utterly slay the Amalekites. Following this, an evil spirit from the Lord troubled him so that his servants brought David to play his harp and soothe his nerves on these occasions. "There is no peace, saith my God, to the wicked" (Isa. 57:21). Saul lost his kingdom, his family, his peace, his glory, his power, his fellowship with Samuel, the man of God, his guidance and his life, on account of his sins.

"Fools make a mock at sin" (Prov. 14:9), but this is a popular game. "It is as sport to a fool to do mischief" (Prov. 10:23), and "a fool layeth open his folly" (Prov. 13:16). "The heart of fools is in the house of mirth" (Eccles. 7:4).

Reflex Effect of Sin

Sin has a reflex effect upon those who engage in it. This is seen in the first chapter of Romans where we read that those who professed themselves to be wise and "became fools and changed the glory of God" were given up by God to receive in themselves "that recompense of their error which was meet." It is foolish to sin, because sin injures one's self, and one is a fool to injure himself.

Second, the man who builds without a foundation plays the

fool. Fools build their character on a foundation of sand. Jesus said, "Therefore, whosoever heareth these sayings of mine, and doeth them, I will liken him unto a wise man, which built his house upon a rock: And the rain descended, and the floods came, and the winds blew, and beat upon that house; and it fell not: for it was founded upon a rock. And every one that heareth these sayings of mine, and doeth them not, shall be likened unto a foolish man, which built his house upon the sand: And the rain descended, and the floods came, and the winds blew, and beat upon that house; and it fell: and great was the fall of it" (Matt. 7:24-27).

How foolish to build without a solid foundation! But that is what is being done in the modern educational system. Some time ago the late Dorothy Thompson related the frank confessions of four college graduates concerning the effects of education on their lives. All were graduated from an old and honored eastern institution. All four had achieved high scholastic records and had won other honors. While the four were all very different from each other, yet each told substantially the same distressing story.

They testified that their education had broken down their belief in positive values; it had weakened their faith in their country and its traditions; it had left them in intellectual confusion and inner despair. They had sought an escape in various ways: one cast his lot temporarily with the Communists; another into complete skepticism and cynicism; another into "the only thing that seemed solid—his own egotism and self-interest."

One boy, who came near to a nervous breakdown and whose family sent him to a psychiatrist before he managed to pull himself together, said, "When I went to college I was full of enthusiasm, particularly interested in history and philosophy. I wanted to find out what made the wheels go around in the world. I wanted to prepare myself to do something—not just make money. I wanted to love something—something bigger than I am—but by my junior year I had become convinced that there wasn't anything that could be believed. Everything was relative, and I was in space. I was like the guy in that poem of Gillett Burgess's:

> I wish that my room had a floor.
> I don't much care for a door.
> But this floating around
> Without touching the ground
> Is getting to be quite a bore.

We need to educate our young people, but we must give them a solid foundation to stand on.

The Fool Leaves God Out

The fool leaves God out of his life. "The fool hath said in his heart, There is no God" (Ps. 53:1). In his head the fool knows that there is a God. The fact of God is an institution. Man knows instinctively and by intuition that there is a God. But "in his heart" the fool says, "No God." The words "there is" are in italics; they are not in the original Hebrew. The fool says, "No God"—that is, "No God for me."

Many people who are not atheists theoretically are practical atheists. An atheist orator on a soapbox said, "There is no God." A good old Christian man at the edge of the crowd said, "He means that he knows uv." There are a lot of practical atheists like the rich fool who "thought within himself" but left God out of his thinking.

God has a will concerning everything in your life. He has a will about where you go to school, whom you marry, where you live, how you make a living, how you conduct yourself every moment. God has a blueprint for your life, and if you are trying to improve on God's plan for your life you are playing the fool.

Third, the person who puts off the most important thing in his life—salvation—and gambles with his immortal soul, plays the fool. If you gain the whole world and lose your soul, you make a poor bargain. You are a fool to trade "an inheritance incorruptible, and undefiled, and that fadeth not away" for an effort to gain this godless world, which no man has ever gained. If you should succeed in gaining the world, it would bring you only one disappointment after another. Then if you *could* gain the world, you could not keep it. You will have to die. And if you did not have to die, you could not keep the world, because some day God will destroy it.

No Lease on Life

"It is appointed unto men once to die" (Heb. 9:27). "Ye shall die like men" (Ps. 82:7). You have no lease on life. It is foolish to put off salvation. This message could be your last warning. Jesus said that the five virgins who were unprepared were foolish virgins. He also told about a man who said to his soul, "Thou hast much goods laid up for many years," but He said that God said unto that man, "Thou fool, this night thy soul shall be required of thee." He was a fool because he thought he had plenty of time.

A Foolish Old Man

The man who puts off the most important matter of life is foolish. I talked with an old man about his need of Christ one night. He said to me, "I heard the Gospel before you were born." I replied, "Then you have put off salvation for a long time. This could be your last call." He said, "Don't worry about me. I know the Gospel. I will be saved before I die, but I am not ready to do it now." I answered with the Bible, "Boast not thyself of to morrow; for thou knowest not what a day may bring forth" (Prov. 27:1). The man became angry and refused to talk. But he died that night at 2 o'clock and went out into a Christless eternity.

Calling Late

In a North Carolina town where I held meetings a man fell from a three-hundred-foot smokestack. On the way to the ground he cried so that he was heard over a mile away, "Lord, have mercy on my soul!" If he cried in faith, his soul bounced right on back to Heaven, for the Bible tells us, "For whosoever shall call upon the name of the Lord shall be saved" (Rom. 10:13). If the man did not call in faith, he kept on going. A man is taking a long chance to put off calling upon God until he is dying. It is a foolish thing to do.

Jesus Knocks at the Door

Oh, how foolish is the mind of man! "The foolishness of God is wiser than men" (I Cor. 1:25). I am free to confess that I was a fool indeed because I turned Jesus away from my heart's door often before that memorable day when, praise God, I let Him come in. He knocked one day, and I said, "Who is there?" He said, "Jesus." I asked, "What do You want, Jesus?" He said, "I want to come in and set things right!" I said, "No, You will spoil my plans and You will kill my joy." My plans needed changing and my joy was empty, but I turned Jesus away. He came back one day and knocked again. I asked, "Who is there?" He answered, "Jesus." "What do You want, Jesus?" "I want to come in and bring salvation to you," He said. But I sent Him away. Then one day He knocked again and I let Him come in. Thank God! I let Him come in.

> He stood at my heart's door in sunshine and rain,
> And patiently waited an entrance to gain;
> What shame that so long He entreated in vain,
> For He is so precious to me.

Just now the Lord Jesus Christ is knocking at your heart's door. He loved you and gave Himself for you. He took all of your sins in His body and died on a cross to pay your penalty of guilt. He now lives and is able to save. "He that hath the Son hath life; and he that hath not the Son of God hath not life" (I John 5:12).

Surely you will not play the fool! Do not go on without Jesus, friend. Do not be so foolish. Open your heart to the risen Christ!

With John and Penny.